Your Key to Self-Knowledge

Use *Astrological Revelations About You* as a key to unlock the mysteries within you and everyone else you *think* you know!

Hollywood's famous "astrologer to the stars," Sydney Omarr, shares his insights to help you understand more about who you really are—and who you can become. You'll discover:

- Crucial information about your character, your life, and the inner you
- Your astrological potential for success and happiness
- Which careers your stars have selected for you
- Your best prospects for friendship and romance
- Your surprising hidden talents

Astrological Revelations About You also lists the birthstone, flower, numbers, color, cities, and countries associated with your sign—plus gives astro-savvy advice to help you hook up romantically with members of any zodiac sign.

This book has already helped thousands of readers reach a new level of self-knowledge—it can help you, too.

About the Author

It would be hard to find any one person who has done more to present astrology to the world than Sydney Omarr. In a career that spans over fifty years, he has spread his mastery of the ancient art via books, newspapers, magazines, radio, television, countless personal consultations—even the internet and telephone services. Movie stars, television celebrities, political figures, and even the U.S. Army have been the beneficiaries of his astonishingly accurate astrological predictions and analysis.

If you know what to say when someone asks "What's your sign?"—you can probably thank Sydney Omarr.

To Contact the Author

If you would like more information about this book, please write in care of Llewellyn Worldwide. All mail addressed to the author is forwarded, but the publisher cannot, unless specifically instructed by the author, give out an address or phone number. Please write to:

Sydney Omarr
c/o Llewellyn Publications
P.O. Box 64383, Dept. K504–5
St. Paul, MN 55164–0383, U.S.A.

Please enclose a self–addressed, stamped envelope for reply or $1.00 to cover costs. If ordering from outside the U.S.A., please enclose an international postal reply coupon.

SYDNEY OMARR

ASTROLOGICAL
REVELATIONS
ABOUT YOU

BARNES
&NOBLE
BOOKS
NEW YORK

Published by MJF Books
Fine Communications
322 Eighth Avenue
New York, NY 10001

Astrological Revelations about You
LC Control Number 03-109432
ISBN 1-56731-593-3

This edition published by arrangement with Llewellyn Publications,
St. Paul, MN 55107
www.llewellyn.com

This book has also been published under the title
Sydney Omarr's Astrological Revelations about You

Manufactured in the United States of America on acid-free paper ∞

MJF Books and the MJF colophon are trademarks of Fine Creative
Media, Inc.

QM   10 9   8 7 6 5 4 3 2 1

Contents

Introduction

A strology today is available to most of us, in contrast to the past, when only kings, rulers, dictators, captains of industry, society leaders, and millionaires were able to delve into what was a hermetically sealed subject.

Now there is a renaissance; books and magazines devoted to astrology flow from the presses; radio programs, recordings, television productions, and motion pictures feature the subject. People speak out; they tell of their interest in this scientific art which has intrigued man from the beginning of recorded history.

The Space Age has moved us closer to the planets. Industry has utilized astrological concepts in the hiring of personnel, the detecting of economic and other cycles, as well as in the forecasting of disturbances to the Earth's ionosphere. Solar flares are predicted through astrological techniques, thus bringing astrology into the race for landings on the Moon and planets. Medical men concede the Moon's apparent influence on moods and even on post-operative blood loss.

Newspapers throughout the world feature astrology columns. Editors, through leadership surveys, are convinced that an astrological description of the day is a "must" as far as their readers are concerned.

Celebrities, whose names are household words throughout much of the world, openly and enthusiastically discuss astrology. Man, in his bid to understand "inner" as well as outer space, has turned to the planets. Astrology supplies the dynamic of time: a time to reap, to sow; astrology enables us to improve the timing of our own moves, our very lives.

People born in different climates, different seasons, are distinguishable. And those born under different zodiacal signs, from Aries to Pisces, possess identifiable characteristics. Nine out of ten persons can tell you under which sign they were born; thus, astrology, like mathematics and music, has become a universal language.

Most people know that a horoscope is a map of the heavens based on month, date, time, and place; almost all know that the Earth takes approximately one year to move around the Sun. This movement, viewed from the Earth, places the Sun in various zodiacal areas during the year. Thus, Barbra Streisand was born when the Sun was in Taurus, while Judy Garland, so typical of her sign, was a Gemini. And you, too, were born when the Sun was transiting one of the twelve zodiacal signs. That, of course, is something all of us have in common; we were all born and we were born under a sign of the zodiac.

Introduction

Through records and studies going back to ancient astrologer-astronomers and reaching forward to current classrooms and laboratories—from Ptolemy to Jung, from Hippocrates to Evangeline Adams—the focus has sharpened on the meaning of your date of birth. Thus, astrology does explore inner space and helps answer the question, "Why am I here?"

Astrology throws light on every department of life; we become enlightened about our activities, actions, reactions. We learn how we respond to others; our secrets as well as our personalities, are revealed. From sex to career to character and future prospects—and more—all are part of astrology's revelations about you.

Through this book, covering every zodiacal sign, it is hoped that further studies will be inspired. But whether one embarks on the road of astrology for entertainment or enlightenment, the journey is rewarding.

In these revelations, you have a key which can open doors to self-knowledge. If you proceed to the locked doors of others—friends, associates, employers, employees, loved ones—you will indeed be in a better position to assume the captaincy of your own destiny. For understanding of each of the zodiacal signs can be a turning point from poverty to a richness of spirit, from ignorance to a warm glow of satisfaction which results when you strike the chord of self-familiarity and tune in on the thoughts, character, and motives of those who share this sojourn.

It is here in this book. There truly is no limit to how high you can reach, how far you can go. The goal is upward and the sky is the limit!

—Sydney Omarr

Aries
March 21 - April 19

Birthstone
Amethyst

Flower
Sweet Pea

Numbers
9, 1, and 8

Color
Red

Part of Body
Head

Cities
Birmingham, Florence,
Naples, Verona, Marseilles

Countries
England, Germany, Israel,
Denmark, Poland, Japan

YOUR CHARACTER AND LIFE

Your inner desires lean toward independence; you want to be free. You are concerned with the kind of freedom which permits you to lead, to pioneer, to be first. You were, as a matter of fact, born under the *first* zodiacal sign and you have basic qualities of leadership. The key is to control, to discipline these qualities; otherwise, a desire to lead could be transformed into arrogant disregard for rules. Learn rules before you break them. That way, Aries, you will be free because with knowledge comes strength.

It is not so much that you want to be in charge; it is that you want to spread out, to be a part of your time, to initiate styles, trends. This is the way you want to lead, this is your way of being strong and free. You aim directly for your mark; your Mars significator is arrow-like. A target is before you and you want the bull's-eye. Some feel you are too direct, and too much the director.

My basic revelation about you is that in actuality you seek strength in others. You admire directness, leadership. These are qualities many attribute to you. But, if the truth be known, these actually are qualities you admire, are drawn to—at times, you take on a kind of "reflection" of what you want to find in a special person. You are, in effect, saying, "Why can't you be this way: Mars-like, Aries-like; be as I would like to be, as I would *want* you to be." Thus, you are apt to confuse what you *seek* with what you are or want to be.

This may sound complicated. But, if you think about it, the picture will clarify; you will see yourself. Here it is, perhaps in plainer words: you "take on" attributes you wish to find in others. You do so in the belief (perhaps mistaken) that by displaying these qualities, you will attract persons who possess them. This doesn't always work. Many times (check recent experiences), in displaying strong leadership, you attract followers. That's not what you really seek; you seek strength, not weakness. You seek one who can lead, not bow; you long for one who can inspire, not be dependent. You are, in this manner, actually embarked on a subconscious search.

You set goals which often appear impossible to achieve. In turn, you expect others to have similar goals. Yet, in this life, concessions are made. You make them and so do others. Because this is so, you tend to feel a lack. There is a vacuum to be filled: with fire, drive, leadership, power that is akin to dictatorial authority. You give the impression of wanting to lead, but you seek a leader. Your planet is Mars and your element is Fire; you crave the excitement of doing, of being in the midst of what is *happening*.

What is happening now is that you are being revealed to yourself through this astrological revelation. You are self-assertive, independent; you stress originality and you want to see how far you can go. On the negative side, you want to see how much you can get away with; you test, experiment, wanting to see what the other person is made of, whether this or that individual is worthy of you (your goals, projections, ideals). The point is that, when you give, you give everything. You are made vulnerable; you know this and seek only the best (in your lights) so that your trust will not be violated. You do not want to waste your emotions, talent, energies; you do not want to give love to one who takes and is not capable of giving in return.

Although you have qualities of leadership, you constantly seek a leader. I've said this before and it is necessary to repeat it. I do this to implant it in your mind and give you a greater chance for self-recognition. If finally you do realize that you want someone who is strong, you will stop trying to break the spirit of those who become important to you. You must learn to encourage, to build, to inspire others to self-confidence. Then, Aries, you will find what you want and you may find that you already have what you seek. It's not as much of a dilemma as you feel it is. In actuality, it is as simple as knowing that you are capable of destroying spirit or creating a flame of inspiration. Put more simply: when you nag, you tear down. When you bicker and complain, you destroy the subtle qualities you seek. When you encourage, you help mold the kind of individual you can respect—and love. With you, respect comes first, followed by love. You simply have to understand that help from you is required if the individual in question is to develop into your kind of "leader." It takes effort and a degree of faith. But, if this lesson sinks in, you are on the road to greater happiness. Some can love first, and respect may or may not come later. That's not the story with you: it is respect first and foremost— then love. Thus, you must help a special person develop self-respect. This will be followed by your respect—and, ultimately, love.

I never said you were not complicated!

Many women born under this sign are determined to find men who can take the reins, call the turns, provide and protect. But very often, the Aries woman attracts a man who is looking for a mother. You can avoid this by encouraging your man to be manly—but not by complaining, finding fault, being impatient. That's a vital revelation. What use you make of it, Aries, is up to you.

Listen, Aries: realize that at times you frighten the very persons you seek to attract. Your pride and, on the negative side, your arrogance, causes some to shy away, to look around and beyond you. Thus, you could wind up with an individual only too willing to follow, to be protected, sheltered, dominated. That's exactly what you do not need! But if you get it, you have only yourself to blame. Absorb what is stated here; what is said could contain a key that opens the way to fulfillment.

Aries, the first sign, is intriguing, fiery, creative, and (as you know) domineering at times. Aries is a wonderful ally, a fighter for a cause, whether it be popular or other- wise. I have met many born under Aries who leave an indelible mark. Among them are Bette Davis, Gloria Swanson, and Jan Sterling. This trio symbolizes the forthrightness, the talent and creative process so apparent in Aries.

I have said about you that what you need, especially if you are a woman, is someone to look up to, to respect. But, before finding this individual, you tend to be aloof. You appear disinterested . . . all the while carefully observing actions, reactions. Now, this does not stem from a desire to deceive. You are not trying to put something over on anyone. Not at all. You do this, Aries, because you are like a princess seeking a frog who will turn into a prince. Fantasy is a very real part of your makeup. You want to approve, to respect, to find someone who is daring, who has initiative. You look, search; your heart is open. But, at the same time, you want to be sure, you want proof.

So you test by being bossy; you test by being critical. And all the time you are secretly hoping the other person will put his foot down, will take over, will assert himself.

You require what might be termed a *heavy amount of affection*. But, with affection, you also need the ingredient of respect. Respect for yourself, for the other individual . . . and unless respect is present, affection and love can fly out of the window.

Men born under Aries are creative, willing to break new ground, to take chances, to invest in their own abilities. But, Aries, you require what might be termed *a private cheering section*. You need someone by your side who appreciates you. You want to share your triumphs with a loved one. Your natural Fifth House—that section of the horoscope associated with love and creative abilities—is Leo. This tells us that you have an insatiable appetite for affection. Now, listen, Aries: it could be said of some persons that they can be smothered by love. But not you. You never get enough of it—not of the right kind.

You are, man or woman, extremely sensitive to loneliness. This being so, you often become *attached* to another individual in what might be termed a *matter of convenience*. You hang on through good times and otherwise. Now, in a positive sense, this is loyalty. In a negative sense, it could be self-punishment. It all depends on *who you are hanging on to,* whether the individual in question is good for you or is hurting you. The key, Aries, is in *knowing when to let go.* Otherwise, you create difficulties for yourself, especially in the love and marriage areas.

Your sign is associated with Mars, and thus most of the problems in your life come when you act on *impulse* and ignore logic. Aries is associated with the head and you tend to be headstrong. But when you combine daring with logic, you are in your element and are most likely to succeed.

Many Aries individuals appear to suffer from eyestrain and give the impression of frowning. Now, Aries, if this applies to you, start practicing your smile. Say "Cheese" if necessary. Do anything to get rid of the frown and to replace it with a come-hither look. Otherwise, you will continue frightening the most worthwhile persons . . . and attracting those apparently destined to hurt you.

You have a way of perceiving the future, of taking the lead. And, Aries, at times your mind is not here with us, but projected into the future. Often you appear to be listening, but actually you are planning your questions, answers, statements, declarations. Unless others understand the real you, they are apt—and understandably so— to think of you as absent-minded, or as a visionary. You see, Aries, you know what it is you want and need—and, often, you skip details, refusing to stop and check the fine print. You get yourself involved with unusual persons, strange situations, and then you sort of shake yourself, and ask *could this be me?* Well, yes, it is you, Aries. That's why I make a point of advising you not to be so headstrong. Wait and observe—try to analyze. Avoid jumping to conclusions. Find the reasons *why*. Don't be satisfied merely that something occurred—find the reason *why*. This will lead to greater self-analysis, and, in turn, to greater self-respect. Now, by this, Aries, I mean that want you to set your sights high . . . not to settle for second best, not to rationalize. In short, Aries, I want you to live up to the best in yourself, to fulfill your potential.

Aries

The late, great astrologer, Grant Lewi, put it this way: *The power of this direct, self-assured approach to life is terrific.* He said: *Being himself, expressing himself, doing according to the needs and dictates of himself, gives Aries a force of personality which, backed by his energy, takes him far, and often fast, along the road of his choice.* And that is a key, Aries. That's why I say: *be yourself—be the best of yourself*—which is mighty hard to top, since you are the first, the leader of the zodiac, the very first House, the first sign—and you are Mars, the planet of action, the spark of accomplishment.

Stop finding reasons for leaning backward to accommodate the desires of others. Please yourself first—then others. Those important to you will also be pleased. There is a difference, Aries, between making intelligent concessions or adjustments, and just plain giving up the battle. Your sign is associated, as we have said, with Mars. This gives you a taste for challenge, for life and for living. You require an air of excitement. But very often, when you find someone you would wish to share this excitement with, that individual is ready to settle down, to fit into a mold, to retire, to stagnate. So you become "pushy"; you push to help that person shake off lethargy. But, as sometimes happens, that person doesn't see the bright side of your pushing, and you are accused of being restless, bossy, of not appreciating what you have at present. Well, Aries, *I don't want you to be merely satisfied.* You're made of stronger stuff! *I want you to fight, challenge, move ahead—to push, if pushing is indeed necessary.*

Look, Aries: you want so much to be understood, to communicate, but you ask, "Where are those who will understand, who will respond?" This leads to a circle—is the good fight worthwhile, is there a chance of winning? Well, Aries, as long as there is effort, a struggle, *there also is a chance.* And being a pioneer, being one who is associated with Mars, the planet of action, *your welfare, your well-being, depends on that fight, depends on action,* and you cannot, must not, give up or lie dormant. I know that you know what I am talking about—you are Aries, the leader, you are first, and you cannot settle for second best. It is first—not second—place that you seek in this personal race, in this competition, in this game of life. Know this, Aries, and respond accordingly.

Don't give in merely for the sake of peace, for harmony; it simply does not work where you are concerned. I have stated—and I repeat—that you have learned, through bitter experience, that giving in does not lead to harmony. It leads, ultimately, to dissension, to an ultimate break in relationships. If you have responded to this negative aspect, you have, very likely, married more than once and beneath your station in life.

As an Aries, you have been described as energetic, enterprising, enthusiastic, impulsive. But unless there is *love* in your life, you tend to become nagging, bitter, striving to be heard in such a manner that you become shrill. So Aries, the less love you have the more you strive for it. And the more you strive, the less likely you are to attain what you seek. What I mean to say is, when love is lacking, you strain, you become tense, you actually stave off what you seek. You become, in a way, ultrasensitive.

You may say, "It is not easy to understand the way Omarr writes about me. There is a kernel of truth, but I want to grasp the entire meaning." All right. Take a deep breath, and listen. It is not easy. I have said in my writings—and I say again here—that each individual is more complicated than the most delicate machinery. But once you understand the *why* of your actions—and the reactions of others—you have the basis for intelligent living, for greater attainment; you have the notes, the score necessary for making each day, for making your life, a song.

Now, Aries, you have universal appeal. That is, your influence, your desires and interests are not confined to a small circle. You reach out and touch the pulse of the public, the heartbeat of your time. That's why you attract so many persons to you with *their* problems. You sacrifice for others, *especially children.* You are sparked by, given life by, your offspring. If you have no children, you adopt, perhaps in a symbolic sense, the children of others. You become concerned, involved. At times you impression that you are "taking over," taking complete charge— instead of merely being helpful and constructively concerned. This happens whether the child in question is a niece, nephew, neighbor's child, or your own offspring.

My colleague, Carl Payne Tobey, has observed that a high ratio of Aries people of both sexes have problems relating to children. He says—and he is an excellent astrologer—that there can be many health problems involving the children, and that Aries is inclined to do all the children's thinking for them. Aries, thus, should be very careful that they do not, in this way, drive their own children away from them when they become adults.

Now, listen, Aries: you are a natural fighter for any cause you think is right. You are headstrong and you are energetic. You ask for no quarter—but, at times, you startle many by giving it. You ask no favors for yourself, but you are lenient with others. You can overcome defeat, rise to your feet, and present an amazing display of second wind. You instill many of us with a zest for life. You make living an adventure.

And listen again: Sometimes you provide such encouragement, you give others such an insight of what *could be, what they could make of themselves,* that they thank you and go on their way to that greater life you made them aware of in the first place, leaving you where you were in the beginning, leaving you alone. And you say: "If only I had known!"

But, Aries, would it have made such a difference? And what if it would have made a difference? The idea is that you must benefit from the *value* of past experience and not brood or speculate about it. The past is past. You are the leader and must look to the future. Think about potential instead of brooding. If you do this, then, Aries, it will be *you* who goes ahead to that greater life, you on the move—not standing still, not compromising, not being left alone with memories.

Aries, you are warm, passionate, generous with your affections. You often startle the opposite sex. This is because, on the surface, you give the appearance of being aloof. But once your confidence is gained, you give and give. At times, this causes others to back off. They tend to be suspicious of your fiery, Martian warmth. "What is the motive?" they ask. Well, you must realize this about yourself, Aries, and the more aware of the effect this part of you has on others.

You are great when it comes to sharing and teaching. You learn by teaching. In fact, Aries, you are better at helping others than at aiding yourself. Obviously, then, you should strive to follow some of your own advice.

You can be militant, determined, and obstinate. And once you get rolling down the wrong road, you tend to remain in motion and in the same direction. You play hard. You work hard. You hate to leave any task, any situation, in an unfinished state. You want to complete—you need to feel completed. You look, search, demand answers.

You have a code, but allow others to break it—which tells us that it is necessary for you to draw a line and keep to it. In other words, don't permit others constantly to take advantage of you.

You are an invigorating, delightful individual, despite the fact that, often, you appear to be frowning. Smile!

You have, the ability to lead, Aries. And *we* want to follow. But first and foremost, the idea is to *lead yourself* to fulfillment. You can do it—we know it and you know it. Now, get going!

THE ARIES LOVER

Now, here are some secret hints, for men only, about Aries women. The Aries woman is not the kind you can lead around in circles. She usually wants to know where you're taking her . . . and she has some ideas of her own on how to get there. She can be temperamental, headstrong, independent, and exude a kind of charm and sex appeal based on a blending of arrogance and pride. You can't force or push the Aries woman, but neither should you fear her.

At least, men, *never let her know you're afraid!* Listen: the Aries woman can stand criticism, so there is no need to worry. In fact, she can stand almost anything—except being ignored.

Here's another valuable hint for men about the Aries woman. Never permit her to think you're an easy catch. Let her work for your approval—make her strive to please you. Admittedly, men, this takes skill on your part . . . but the results will be worth the time and trouble!

Now, here is a special tip for women about the Aries man: keep his ego up. Once he begins to lag or sag, he is heading for trouble. See to it that the Aries man gets plenty of exercise and encouragement. Tell him how good he is; good as a person, good in his professional endeavors, good as a lover. If you make him feel this is true— *it becomes so.* The more be thinks you appreciate him, the more the Aries man will return the compliment.

Being interested in an Aries man or woman is like taking a new lease on life. These people revitalize all of us.

YOUR RISING SIGN

All persons born under your sign are not exactly the same, although basic characteristics will hold. A horoscope, in actuality, is a map of the sky based on the time and place of birth. One of the most important parts of the horoscope is the Rising Sign, which is the sign coming up over the eastern horizon when you were born. It's best to get a birth chart to be sure of the sign, but if you know your birth time, here is your probable Rising Sign and some variations it may cause in your life and character:

Aries

Born between 4:00 and 6:00 A.M., the Aries qualities are intensified, because it is likely that your Rising Sign also is Aries. Thus, the Mars influence is doubled. It's important that you check a tendency to be overly aggressive. Your pioneering instincts are magnified; you want to be there first and to build, build, until your mark, your style, your imprint is indelible. In so doing, be sure you are working with available material, not counting on something which does not actually exist. Many comment that you take too many chances, but, with you, that's the name of the game: taking a chance, the daring, the initiative, the spirit required to begin and end, to finish and start anew. You are headstrong, at times domineering; but also a humanitarian and a natural fighter for the underdog.

Born between 6:00 and 8:00 A.M., your Ascendant or Rising Sign is likely to be Taurus, making Venus the ruler or significator of your chart. Venus and Mars (your Sun sign ruler) combine to make you vitally attractive to the opposite sex. The Taurus Ascendant takes some of the "sharp edge" off your Sun in Aries. You are sensuous, in love with love, the kind of person who (once in love) will strive to build a home, an empire, all for the sake of lover, mate, children. This combination, however, could also cause a pugnacious streak; you are stubborn, daring, willing to stick your chin out for family, mate, or lover. You are more practical than the average Aries individual, and you also have a greater knack of acquiring wealth. Control your temper—and you could end up controlling a powerful and wealthy organization.

Aries

Born between 8:00 and 10:00 A.M., your Rising Sign, very likely, is Gemini, giving Mercury as significator of your Ascendant. Mercury combines with your Mars Solar ruler to add to your versatility. With Gemini rising, you are more restless than is the usual Aries native. You are willing to make changes, to experiment: you puncture stuffed shirts, and are a natural enemy of pomposity. You are attracted to the fields of writing, photography, teaching. You ask questions and are persistent enough to obtain answers. You are apt to do much traveling, make numerous contacts—and, at times—love more than one person simultaneously. You are more animated than is the classic Aries; you become involved in situations which test your skill and mental resources. The odds are that you will, on most occasions, land on your feet.

Born between 10:00 A.M. and 12:00 noon, your Rising Sign is likely to be Cancer, associated with the Moon. This gives you more of an interest in future security, home and family. Your moods vary; you exhibit a tendency to vacillate. You are more receptive than is the usual Aries individual. Your appearance, too, could be different: a slight tendency toward a "moon face," a tendency, also, to put on weight. Your concern with home and family welfare is intensified. It could also come out in a parochial attitude about schooling, the city, the state. Your views, thus, could become extreme or narrow. You build a protective emotional shell, become engrossed in genealogy, or concerned with family history when, perhaps, your time could be more profitably utilized in planning ahead.

Aries

Born between 12:00 noon and 2:00 P.M., your Rising Sign is apt to be Leo, associated with the Sun. This indicates a sparkling personality, makes you more gregarious than is the average person born under Aries. You have in excellent sense of showmanship; you are able to dramatize beliefs. With Leo rising, your sense of humor and dynamic approach to persons and situations are also accented. You tend to be more restless than is true of most Arians. Your qualities of independence and your original approach are highlighted. You are a natural executive because others are inspired by your drive and the "power" you seem capable of emanating. You must avoid permitting determination to deteriorate into mere obstinacy. You are able to sway people—and you could lead others to success and prosperity.

Born between 2:00 and 4:00 P.M., your Rising Sign is likely to be Virgo, giving Mercury as ruler of your Ascendant. The combination of your Mars Solar significator with Mercury makes you inquisitive. You are never satisfied merely to know something happened; you want the reasons, you want to know *why* it occurred. At times, you become impatient. Your ideas race ahead of your actions. You feel others should be able to "catch on" quickly, which is not always the case. You exhibit an unusual amount of dexterity, and would make an excellent public speaker. You highlight appearance, are health-conscious, much concerned about youthful concepts, and strive to be "modern." You are more precise than is the average person born under Aries.

Aries

Born between 4:00 and 6:00 P.M., your Rising Sign is apt to be Libra, ruled by Venus. The combination of Venus and your Mars significator emphasizes your desire to lead, direct, to balance, to make decisions having to do with the general welfare of the family. You are artistic, creative, more diplomatic than is the average native of Aries. You possess an awareness of social conditions. It is difficult for you to be happy when others around you are miserable. You are not a good "exploiter." If a bargain is obtained at the expense of another individual, then you do not consider it a legitimate bargain. This causes some of your associates to claim you are impractical. However, it is best for you to adhere to principles and to live by the Golden Rule. The path upward, for you, includes the welfare of others.

Born between 6:00 and 8:00 P.M., your Rising Sign is likely to be Scorpio, associated with Pluto. This combines with your Mars Sun sign ruler to make you intense, more so than is the average native of Aries. When you decide something is to be done, it is all the way—nothing halfway where you are concerned. You tend to break through red tape; it is difficult to fence you in. You are very attractive to the opposite sex; you attract situations which could be considered bizarre. You are passionate in almost everything you do; you enter projects wholeheartedly. One might say there isn't a lukewarm bone in your body. Many consider you somewhat mystic, and many people seem to think you have a key to getting rich.

Born between 8:00 and 10:00 P.M., you are likely to have Sagittarius as your Ascendant, with Jupiter as a ruling planet. This combines with the Aries Mars to make you somewhat visionary. Your ideals are as real to you as a chair or a loaf of bread. You are sustained by humanitarian projects; your desire is to have a far-reaching effect on people, places and events. You are restless, energy-filled, capable of influencing large groups. At times you scatter your forces. You try to do too many things at once. It is not unusual for you to read three books at a time, or to attempt to write more than one during the same time period. With this Sagittarius-Aries combination, you could be considered egotistical. This is because you seem indifferent to petty happenings. You are more concerned with the large picture, causing some to regard you as aloof.

Born between 10:00 P.M. and 12:00 midnight, your Ascendant is likely to be Capricorn, ruled by Saturn. The Capricorn-Aries (Mars) combination is powerful; the ingredient of ambition is accented. You have drive and staying power. Your sense of timing is better than can be claimed by the average Aries native. You are capable of assuming responsibility; you are confident that time will justify your beliefs, methods. Some claim you are too serious, too much concerned with ultimate goals, even with your place in history. But that is the way you are; you feel destined to make a mark. Aries gives you the fire, the drive, while Capricorn provides a quality of permanency. You are here to stay; your words, actions (however impulsive they may appear) are designed for overall, even *historic* effect.

Born between 12:00 midnight and 2:00 A.M., your Rising Sign is likely to be Aquarius, ruled by Uranus. The combination of this planet and your Aries Mars adds to the excitement you generate with your presence. You are altruistic, liberal, concerned with the future—perhaps much more so than with today. You are in excellent organizer; you can bring together persons of divergent views. You do exhibit a tendency to be impulsive. But, on the positive side, this makes you daring and causes the opposite sex to describe you as "dashing." You are inventive, fascinated with electronics, television. Your personality is compelling, and people gravitate to you. You constantly strive for greater freedom of expression. Not everyone agrees with you, but few can forget what you do or say.

Born between 2:00 and 4:00 A.M., your Rising Sign is likely to be Pisces, giving Neptune as your significator. This, combined with your Aries-Mars, creates something of a contradiction in your makeup. You are, on the one hand, a dreamer. On the other, you are an individual of action. If you successfully blend Mars and Neptune, you act to make dreams become realities. You succeed when you apply yourself to *defining intangibles.* You would make an excellent researcher in the fields of ESP and psychic phenomena. Also, you are capable of succeeding in motion pictures and television; this represents the bringing of illusion to the screen, a perfect example of dreams combined with reality. Your ideas are peculiarly your own—you cannot depend on approval from the majority. You must continue to be unique; you should avoid brooding if your efforts don't gain immediate acceptance.

ARIES FRIENDS AND PARTNERS

Aries is harmonious in relation to Leo, Sagittarius, Aquarius, and Gemini. With another Aries, the relationship is one that is active, constantly striving idealistic, concerned with universal appeal and faraway places. It could be quite fiery; both would want to assume leadership. Aries is not favorably aspected to Libra, Cancer, or Capricorn. Aries can be considered neutral where the following signs are concerned: Taurus, Virgo, Scorpio, and Pisces.

ARIES CAREERS

Of course, an analysis of your complete horoscope (month, date, year, hour, and place of birth) is required for a definitive statement on your vocation. However, with the knowledge that your natal Sun was in Aries, it is possible to gain an overall picture of the indications for your career.

You are capable of assuming responsibility, and have the inner drive necessary to be a good executive. Your qualities of natural leadership become evident in any chosen career or occupation.

When you exude confidence, you attract support from people with money and authority. Where your profession is concerned, you are serious. You want to utilize your own style, leave your mark, build on your ideas.

The Tenth House is associated with career; that sector of your Solar horoscope contains Saturn—ruled by Capricorn. Utilize your drive; transpose your energy into power. It is not necessary to be domineering, but you must express your views. Time is on your side; you utilize experience better than does the average individual. You are not likely to make the same mistake twice.

You are capable of protecting assets; you seldom give products away for nothing. You are a good horse-trader. You are able to perceive *future values.* You are not afraid to wait; time usually is on your side. Your acumen about investments is highlighted; when you put time in, it is not merely to waste minutes and hours. There is usually a purpose, a sense of direction to your efforts.

In your career, patience can become your greatest asset, while impulsiveness could be the forerunner to loss. Your way to success is through a combination of independence, initiative and a willingness to wait. Learn to be patient, and limit your moves.

You are a natural executive. You would make an excellent army officer, iron or steel authority, police chief, hardware manufacturer, or politician. Many actors and actresses were born under Aries; you may have the drive to succeed in this area, too. You could excel as a facial beauty expert. You possess qualities which would also fit in well with the following occupations: dentist, physician, advertising director, public relations specialist, armament maker.

THE ARIES HAND

Some astrologers are proficient at guessing Sun signs; that is, they can look at an individual and perceive his, or her, zodiacal sign. This is no easy task—it requires experience, practice. The reason is that the Rising Sign (at the time and place of birth) affects personality and appearance, as does the sign the Moon occupied at birth. Yet, the place of the

Sun is a strong indicator where character and appearance enter the picture.

Over the years, I have found that one significant key in this effort is the human hand. A person's hand often reveals whether that individual was born under a Fire, Earth, Air, or Water Sign.

You, Aries, were born under a Fire Sign; Aries belongs to the Fire element. The Fire Sign group (which includes Aries, Leo, and Sagittarius), in a majority of cases, appear to have cone-shaped hands. The hands are comparatively small, with the palms larger than the fingers, and broad at the base, tapering toward the fingers. This group can also be distinguished by high foreheads. There is tendency for the hair to recede, giving an intellectual appearance.

Your hands are quite expressive; your general appearance could be described as striking.

ARIES SECRETS

The horoscope, with its twelve angles or Houses, covers every area of life, including your secrets. The Twelfth House holds sway over secret fears, fantasies, undercover problems, all that is hidden or beneath the surface. In your case, Pisces occupies your Twelfth House. The Neptune of Pisces combines with your Mars significator to emphasize fantasy. One of your basic secrets is a fear of uncertainty. You tend to be a victim of self-doubt. To cover up, you often put on a display of arrogance, of certainty, of missionary zeal.

Another of your basic worries is a fear that your secrets will be exposed. Your secrets are woven with your fears about not being perfect. More than most persons, you are on guard against embarrassment. Some can make mistakes and go on, realizing that to err is human. Not so with you; mistakes, mishaps are personal. Rejection is not regarded on an impersonal or objective plane; with you, this amounts to an attack on your basic security.

Now, listen: realize that perfection could be an unattainable goal. Your ideas will not always meet with an enthusiastic reception. This should not, in your mind, reflect on the validity of those ideas. You often are a pioneer, ahead of your time. Thus, it is natural that some friends and associates will be puzzled by your proposals.

You are extremely sensitive and this makes you vulnerable to insults, ridicule, emotional barbs. One of your secrets is a desire to reveal only what you feel should be made known. You feel you have privileged information, and can be discreet to the point of no return. This means that, at times, you can put on a hard or "tough" front: but, inwardly, you are filled with doubts—about religion, personal capabilities, convictions. To overcome this, you often resort to excess speed—and this could make you accident-prone.

Listen: the greatest antidote for your secret fears is a realistic attitude. See persons, situations as they actually exist—not merely as you *wish* they could be.

Your secret is really your degree of sensitivity. You are a romantic. You want perfection, you even *expect* it. Thus, your own flaws and the flaws of others are, to your way of thinking, to be "covered up." In so doing, you could hide qualities of value.

A secret affair, a secret business transaction—these, too, are part of your Twelfth House makeup. Another inner conviction, or secret feeling, is the "I really do know best" one. This syndrome creates friction. Realize, Aries, that what you *think* you know is not actually always correct. There is room for error, for correction. When this point is made, you will no longer be so harshly embarrassed by rebuffs, real or imagined.

It is within the realm of possibility that you secretly write poetry. This is constructive. But if you insist on keeping it a secret, it could develop into a fetish. You would find it helpful to maintain a diary. This provides a healthy outlet; then your thoughts are placed on paper, in an orderly fashion.

Don't be ashamed of your secrets; most of them, if the truth be known, are shared by a good number of other perfectly normal, healthy persons.

Taurus
April 20 – May 20

Birthstone
Emerald

Flower
Lily of the Valley

Numbers
6, 4, and 2

Colors
Blue and Pink

Parts of Body
Throat and Neck

Cities
Dublin, Leipzig, Mantua,
St. Louis

Countries
Ireland, Cyprus, Greece

YOUR CHARACTER AND LIFE

Yours is the second sign of the zodiac. It intrigues, sometimes puzzles, and causes astrologers to argue. Some insist you are stubborn, indolent. Others brush that charge aside and say you appreciate the good life, that you are merely resting so as to gain strength with which to enjoy a joust with life. Many claim you are possessed of an evil temper; others claim it is only when someone waves a red flag in front of the bull, as it were, that your temper rises.

Obviously, the truth is somewhere in between. Like Cancer, you are quite aware of money. Money, when it comes, is used to luxuriate. You can be irritable with persons who display lack of knowledge, class, or general quality. You have little patience with those who claim to be authorities and act as if they were amateurs. Luxurious Venus is the ruler of Taurus, so you have a great appreciation of beauty, and you also love the fine things in life. Luxury delights you. Some people have a guilt complex about enjoying luxuries, but not you. You enjoy, appreciate, develop an appetite for them.

At times you appear to be immobile—not able to move, wanting to remain, to stay, to have the world stand still, to have problems walk away while you watch, rest, and contemplate. Taurus is a fixed sign of the Earth element— it contributes to a tendency toward obstinacy and an appreciation of the basics: eating, drinking, loving.

Here is a revelation about you: you enjoy periods of silence. This bothers some—they want you to talk, they want you to appear animated. If this is what they want so much, they should find themselves a Gemini!

As for you, periods of self-contemplation are as necessary as food and water. Learn to appreciate the need for these periods of reflection. But, Taurus, also reassure those close to you that this is not a means of sulking or of showing lack of interest. Make it easier for others to understand. After all, silence can be a potent weapon. If you utilize it in this sense, it's no wonder that others cringe in the face of it. But if it is understood that this is a period of personal reflection, then no one (who is reasonable) could object.

Taurus rules the throat, and it is interesting to note how many singers were born under this sign: Bing Crosby, Patrice Munsel, Anna Maria Alberghetti, Carol Burnett, Kate Smith, and many others. Irving Berlin exemplified the Taurus sense of music, to say nothing of Harry Truman! The Taurean often has an unusual speaking voice: James Mason, Orson Welles, and Raymond Burr, to mention but a few of the numerous celebrities born under your sign.

Often, you are not the same "inside" as your outward manner would lead one to believe. To me, a typical Taurus is Perry Como. When I discussed his horoscope with him, I made it plain that although he appeared quiet, relaxed on the outside, he could seethe inwardly. He verified that what I told him was correct: he can be tense beyond what might be expected of an artist. This can, according to his horoscope, be a problem. The millions who have viewed his relaxed performances might find this difficult to believe, which is a tribute to Como's artistry—and to the accuracy of my astrological analysis (if I may be permitted to take a Leo-like bow).

Taurus, I would like to see you become more flexible. You tend to fix your mind on one object, one objective;

you aim toward that goal as if there were to be no tomorrow. You don't want to be distracted, especially where *money* enters the picture. Taurus is the natural Second House, which is associated with income potential, personal possessions. You delight in obtaining a bargain, although you will gladly exhibit extravagance when it comes to a comfort-producing luxury.

Many who call you obstinate are not aware that the fixed quality of your sign causes you, at times, to fear change. You advocate it for others, but are reluctant when it comes to a transformation of your own personal patterns. Yet, once you do make a decision, a basic change, you often are most happy. What makes you *appear* stubborn, thus, is actually a reluctance which turns to fright when you contemplate what change could entail, what new or different circumstances could bring to your life—or take away from it.

Listen: you are tenacious and loyal, but the question is, what are you being loyal to? Are you directing your energies in a constructive manner? You seem to have a knack for tying yourself to persons, situations which can be destructive. Correct this; don't obscure vision by feeling that once you have started doing something one way, that one way is the only way. It is not. Open your mind to a *sense of experimentation*.

You can be extremely affectionate—almost grasping. You hate to let go of anything you think you own; but the irony is that, in actuality, you don't own anything, or anyone. To get away from metaphysical terms and come down to earth, you can be too possessive. You have to learn to let go . . . to give others breathing room. Otherwise, you invite rebellion and the very change that you often fear.

I want you to throw off sluggishness. I want you to *get going*. We know, Taurus, that you are your own greatest enemy. If events are going in your favor, you want them always to go in the same direction. All right. This is natural. No one can blame you for that or find fault with you for wanting the best of everything. But what you must avoid is reluctance to look to the future, to be prepared for change, to be ready with alternative plans . . . to think creatively. Creative thinking, Taurus, equals willingness to change. Once you have the facts, make decisions based on those facts.

At times you appear to be saying, "Don't confuse me with the facts—my mind is made up." This, of course, leads to a rut.

Listen: you were born under a fixed, earthy sign. You appreciate the arts, you are steady, loyal, sympathetic, generally kind—but, Taurus, you must stop *being frightened of change*. Creative thinking encourages change, leaves room for travel, for variety, prepares you for the complexities of life.

Taurus is associated with the neck and throat. Sex, warmth, and love play paramount roles in your life. The late, great astrologer Evangeline Adams said of Taurus: *In their love affairs such people may begin with the vehemence of gales, storm followed by storm. When this passes, the end comes not by breach or tragedy, but by the development of warm friendships. The disposition*, said Miss Adams, *is thus ideal for marriage.*

But I would add this: when roused, when you feel you have been taken advantage of, that placid nature of yours is transformed. The bull goes into a rage. This brings us to another revelation—you tend to go to extremes. Either you are quiet and satisfied, or a raging bull.

The sign on the Fifth House of your Solar horoscope is Virgo. This tells us that, at times, you can be overcritical of loved ones. You can harp and pick, find fault, analyze until what was love turns into something less, much less. Listen, Taurus: you can be very tolerant of strangers, of mere acquaintances, even of friends. But once your emotions are affected, you take a new, different, discriminating look. You are not aware that you are destroying. You think merely that you are being a constructive critic. But, before you know it, you are finding fault . . . and the thing you love, the person you adore, is no longer on a pedestal, but is being slowly torn down and driven away from you. That's why, Taurus, you often are your own worst enemy.

You tell yourself, it is because I love her, or him. You say it is because you really care that you are so observant, so alert to faults. But, Taurus, in becoming ultracritical of those you love, you are, in effect, tearing down your own happiness. The mature, positive Taurean gives his or her all, expresses loyalty in a constructive sense, helps and loves loved ones. But, in the negative sense, you tear, rush, go flying after the red flag, seeking to do away with flaws. But I tell you, Taurus, in doing this, there is danger that you will do away with love completely. I say this: treat loved ones as well as you do acquaintances and you will be on the road to greater emotional security—to greater happiness and to a greater sense of fulfillment.

Taureans must learn to battle fear. The greatest asset in this battle is love. Taurus requires love. Taurus must feel earth beneath the feet. Taurus must be on solid ground.

But when there is a temporary change, a lift or a drop, Taurus must learn to accept, to take this in stride, to ride with the tide, to accept help. Taurus is able to attract allies from the most unexpected sources.

In studying your sign, I have found that once you have proven you know something, once you can accomplish something, you tend to lose interest and let it slide. You tend to become careless.

You gain only to lose. You love only to chase love. You achieve only to fail. Now why this should be is a question you must answer from *within*. Obviously, you require greater self-discipline. You must distinguish between love and lust. You must be aware that sex is a part of love, but not the entire spectrum, not the complete story. Listen, Taurus: you are basically primitive where emotions are concerned. You are capable of making loved ones unhappy by shutting yourself in. You have an enormous emotional shell which you occasionally trot out and cover yourself with. This makes it almost impossible to communicate with you. You are hidden, protected, insulated. At these times it is difficult for you even to communicate with yourself. You see, Taurus, you think you are hiding from the outside. *But you also hide from yourself.* You become a person who can hear only the sound of your own heart beating. The rhythm of self becomes all-engulfing, and what is outside—such as the world, loved ones, emotions—becomes foreign.

You need help at these times; you need to communicate. But the more others try to get through, to touch you, to evoke response, the more difficult you are apt to become, closing in even tighter, clamping shell on shell over yourself and hiding your head as though you were a turtle. Now, listen Taurus: when you overcome this "turtle tendency," you will be on the way to finding greater strengths, a more satisfying life—and greater love.

You are at your best when it is necessary. Which means, Taurus, that you require challenge. When things are too easy, you tend to be lazy. When you have everything your way, you become careless. You tend to tear down what you build. You do this so that you can create the challenge all over again. It is an interesting psychological point and I have found that it specifically applies to you. You do something, perhaps without consciously realizing it, to get yourself going again. You *don't want change,* but *you need it.* You don't welcome challenge, but you require it. Now, listen: you can withstand hardship, overcome obstacles. You are attractive to the opposite sex. You have many remarkable qualities: *build* on these instead of destroying them.

Since Taurus is associated with the throat, the neck, the voice, you could possess an unusual speaking or singing voice. Your physical structure, no matter what your weight, appears formidable. Many Taureans are thick-necked and broad-shouldered. Joe Louis was born under this sign, as was Sonny Liston. One weakness is a tendency to overindulge in food or drink.

You are a great ally, and enjoy a good fight. It is necessary for you to find a *constructive* outlet for your energies. Otherwise, you become so engrossed with yourself you are like one who makes a fetish of body building, of accumulating material things . . . and then you begin to wonder, "What am I going to do with all of this?" Then the circle starts spinning: you collect only to spend, you spend only to collect . . . and so on and on.

Your curiosity is great. It is of the earthy variety, which embarrasses some persons. You are interested in the natural functions of the body. You like to experiment, and your object is pleasure, satisfaction. But you have a tendency to become what might he termed a lazy lover. That is, you seek pleasure but, at times, neglect to give it. This is a sort of Taurus letdown . . . and your mate may wonder, "Whatever happened to that man (or woman) I used to know?"

You feel that you have such great capabilities that there is no necessity for proving yourself. This is negative. It tends to keep you fixed, in a rut. Then you view someone else's success and you are resentful, saying, "That should have been me . . . it could have been me." Check yourself when you feel this resentment. Get your feet solidly on the ground. Face issues as they exist, not the way you feel they should have been. Once you do this, Taurus, then use your talents, and things will begin to be as you *feel* they should be.

Realize that you cannot live on self-love. You require friends, admirers, even adulation. It is best to combine your practical nature with idealism. You can collect facts and figures, but mere statistics lack real meaning for you. You need warmth. You need to learn to love loved ones instead of criticizing them.

Taking the easy way out may seem best, but it simply is not for Taurus. You need the challenge; the spark must be ignited, inertia must give way to action.

You are basically conservative . . . and sensitive. This being the case, you may feel sensitive about some of the things I've said about you. But I also know this: you are gifted with a finely honed sense of truth. You eventually choose truth. Your shoulders are broad, and you are capable of using them for more than mere physical show. You are capable of carrying your own weight, of accomplishing what must be accomplished. You can move in and absorb experience. You can refine what you experience and utilize it to your advantage.

The late, great astrologer Grant Lewi said of you: *The Taurus feels at home, strong and self-assured, when acting according to what he senses within himself. Truth to Taurus is the truth of his own feelings—and unshakable faith in the truth and inevitability of his own feelings constitute his ideals.*

You see, Taurus, you are a basic person in your needs, demands, requirements. You get into difficulty only when you complicate issues.

It is likely that you succeed when close to the earth—when gardening, for example. You have a green thumb and, as Grant Lewi once pointed out, you derive solace, strength, relaxation, and comfort from physical contact with the earth.

Keep your goals in view. Continue to be earthy without being coarse. Be direct without being offensive. Know the truth without castigating others for not seeing the truth as you view it. Loosen the reins. Permit yourself room to love—and to be loved. You can be a happy person, Taurus. *And the only person standing in your way is you!*

You create your own world, be it a city, town, community, patch of land, apartment, or room. You can be silent for hours, which could prove frustrating to one emotionally involved. You can use silence as an ally, a weapon, or a protective shield. I would like to see you more considerate—realize one close to you suffers in your silence. And it is a cruel weapon which eventually could boomerang. Think about it, Taurus. It is fine to contemplate, but negative to use silence as a security blanket. It makes you not a philosopher, but more like a pouting child.

The Taurus Lover

Here is a special hint for men about the women of this sign: the Taurus woman is hungry for experience as well as for food. She wants to taste life. Taurus women are earthy in temperament. There is a tendency for them to become careless about the way they look. When you first meet them, their taste is impeccable. But there is a tendency for them to let themselves run down. They become sure of you—you become one of their possessions. (And Taurus women are fond of possessing!) Well, make sure you are treated as well as a stranger would be. Don't be a stuffed shirt, but refuse to put up with curlers in the hair and a rumpled manner of dress or personality. Listen, men: know when to draw the line at giving in to the whims of the Taurus woman. At times, like a crying baby, she will test you to see just how much she can get away with. Let her go so far—then call a halt. After the obligatory resistance, she'll actually appreciate it. That's the way to get along with the Taurus woman!

Now, here are some tips for women about the Taurus man. He will not appreciate being buried in details, footnotes, resolutions. The best course for the Taurus man is direct, simple. This man likes luxury, but he wants to be practical about it. He wants the best but is not above grumbling about the cost. He admires style, but he wants a woman who can keep an eye on the budget.

Don't try to corral the Taurus man. He wants plenty of room—and lots of love. The more desirable you appear—and the harder you are to get—the more the Taurus man will want you.

The Taurus man can be stubborn. When he makes up his mind to go along a certain path, it is difficult, if not impossible, to make him change. The Taurus man has to be won over with kindness, even guile. He is not always easy to live with. He enjoys the basic things: eating, sleeping, loving, fighting—and if you're looking for perfection, I would advise you to by-pass the Taurus man. But if you desire a very human man . . . then go full speed ahead. And remember—he needs love with a capital "L."

YOUR RISING SIGN

All persons born under your sign are not exactly the same, although basic characteristics will hold. A horoscope, in actuality, is a map of the sky based on the time and place of birth. If you are aware of your birth time, here are some variations it may cause in your life and character:

Born between 4:00 and 6:00 A.M., your Rising Sign is apt to be Taurus, accentuating the Venus qualities, adding to your sense of beauty and highlighting your durability. Your desire for security is magnified; you collect and file, utilizing information for financial gain. Some astrologers insist that you have a green thumb where finances are concerned, especially in the field of real estate. You can "spot" property that is to increase in value. You are versatile, capable of making things grow, including a bank account. Develop your sense of humor; you have, but you have to call on it more often. Or perhaps one should say, you must let it bubble to the surface without choking it down. A sense of humor helps you to attain those basic goals you seek.

Born between 6:00 and 8:00 A.M., your Rising Sign is probably Gemini. The Mercury of this sign combines with your Venus Solar ruler to make you mentally active. Your intuition is more highly developed than the average native of Taurus. You have the ability to sense trends, to get the feel of public reaction. You are active, tend to be nervous. You talk more than most Taureans. Your interests are varied; at times you become concerned with too many subjects at once. You are restless, genial, with an ability to sway people through writing and oratory. At times, however, talk replaces action, short notes substitute for developed themes. The key is to concentrate, to finish what you start, and to share knowledge. Which means exchanging thoughts by developing them until a philosophy emerges.

Born between 8:00 and 10:00 A.M., your Ascendant or Rising Sign is likely to be Cancer, associated with the Moon. The combination of your Venus Solar ruler and the Moon makes you practical, especially where money and security are concerned. You are attracted to the stock market, to banking, to business and finance. You are house-proud. Your home is your castle—and this is more than just a saying with you. You can be stubborn in the sense that once embarked on a theme, a program, you are reluctant to change. You are a good provider and a protector of family and property. You have plenty of ability, probably along more than one line. And you are not alone—you have allies. You are a formidable foe and a valuable ally.

Born between 10:00 A.M. and 12:00 noon, your Rising Sign is likely to be Leo, ruled by the Sun. The Sun-Venus (your Solar significator) combination could create a desire for luxury that is difficult to fulfill. Your tastes are definite—nothing halfway. You are determined, fixed in views, demanding of attention and loyalty, and very attractive to the opposite sex. Your sense of drama is highly developed. When you walk into a room, others are aware of your presence. You like to be recognized, whether by waiters or the public. You are romantic, creative, and more extravagant than is the average Taurean. You are a charming person, and you appear easygoing. However, if someone is looking for a tough adversary, they've found it in you.

Born between 12:00 noon and 2:00 P.M., your Ascendant is probably Virgo, ruled by Mercury. The combination of Venus and Mercury enhances your critical faculties. You are able to perceive, to analyze, to find the *why* of events. You like to think of yourself as being practical, but your intellectual curiosity takes you into areas most persons regard as "far out." You delight in gaining knowledge of generally obscure subjects—and of imparting that information. Thus, you enjoy teaching. But you are not satisfied to know what everyone knows; you prefer the subtle, the specialty. You are not above showing off this knowledge in a manner to cause others to feel a lack in their education. On the positive side, though, you enhance, fill in blanks, and help others to develop a greater variety of interests.

Born between 2:00 and 4:00 P.M., your Rising Sign is likely to be Libra, associated with Venus, the planet which is also your Sun Sign significator. This makes you more of a social animal than most Taureans. You enjoy art, drama; you attract those with creative abilities. You have a special talent for bringing together people with divergent points of view. You are an excellent host or hostess, capable of bringing out the best in others. At times you exhibit a tendency to reflect rather than to take direct action. You know what should be done, but you delay, seemingly content to be comfortable rather than active. It's very important that you utilize your creative abilities: write, sculpt, paint, express yourself. Then life becomes a song rather than mere sing-song.

Born between 4:00 and 6:00 P.M., your Ascendant is probably Scorpio, associated with Pluto. The combination of Pluto and Venus makes you more direct than the average native of Taurus. You have drive, power; you are a self-starter, independent and original. Your appreciation of the basic is great; you are passionate, determined, intuitive. Scorpio rising makes you an individual who draws persons of opposite views. This is because you enjoy conflict, especially a clash of ideas. You are aggressive; you tend to be jealous. When you love, it is all the way. And you will fight for what you believe is right. Basically, you enjoy creature comforts, and your emotions often rule logic. If you can learn to control impulsive actions, you will channel power and enhance your chances for success.

Born between 6:00 and 8:00 P.M., your Rising Sign is probably Sagittarius, ruled by Jupiter. This combines with your Venus to give you a universal view—and appeal. You are more fond of travel than is the average native of Taurus. You draw people to you with their problems. You are interested in the healing arts, in psychology, philosophy, and religion. You are concerned with the traditions of people in foreign lands, and with elevating the standards of those you consider oppressed. You would make an excellent fund-raiser for charities; theater benefit performances succeed with you at the helm. You view projects as a whole but often neglect details. Some humorously refer to you as an "absent-minded professor."

Born between 8:00 and 10:00 P.M., it is likely that your Rising Sign is Capricorn, associated with Saturn. This combines with your Venus to make you more analytical than the average Taurean. You stick with a subject until you know it; you ask questions until answers are obtained. Your love of art objects takes on a practical side; you collect and catalog. You are analytical. Your sense of responsibility is highly developed. You are practical where ultimate goals are concerned. You have a way of getting what you need. Your great ally is a willingness to wait—know this and utilize patience. Some think you are too serious, but many people are envious because you are attractive and successful. You seldom do anything except for a good reason. You plan, conceive, and build; you structure your ideas in a way similar to an architect.

Born between 10:00 P.M. and 12:00 midnight, your Rising Sign is probably Aquarius, associated with Uranus. Combined with your Venus, this makes you a distinctive individual. You are striking, unique, attractive. You are

inventive and possess an abundance of personal magnetism. You delve into a variety of subjects, and you are
capable of transforming interests and hobbies into profitable enterprises. You are anything but ordinary, and your
unique touch dramatizes everyday activities. You enjoy
entertaining; you draw friends, many of whom help you
fulfill hopes and wishes. You have a knack of attracting
those who want to help. You would excel in public relations. Your success comes in an unusual manner: recognition for qualities which you often take for granted.

Born between 12:00 midnight and 2:00 A.M., your Rising
Sign is likely to be Pisces, ruled by Neptune. The combination of Neptune and Venus is a romantic one. You are
willing to break with tradition for what you desire. Many
consider you unorthodox, but, with you, affairs of the heart
take precedence over material matters. You are willing to
build on a dream. Ideas and ideals predominate. You could
find yourself out on a limb, however, if you imagine persons and situations in a manner that is totally divorced
from reality. You are somewhat of a mystic, a poet, one
who is attracted to ESP, psychic phenomena. You fear
being "closed in." You want room to expand your thoughts
and activities. You are practical about being impractical—
which means that you deliberately create an aura of mystery and romance. If not carried to extremes, this adds up
to charm and makes you a most intriguing person.

Born between 2:00 and 4:00 A.M., your Rising Sign likely
to be Aries, ruled by Mars. Combined with your Venus,
this makes you an invigorating person, more direct, active,
and independent than is the average native of Taurus. You

usually take the initiative—and some complain that you are too insistent on having your own way. Your enthusiasm, however, is catching—it doesn't take long for you to convince others to follow your pattern. You work for an objective; when there is a goal it is difficult to dissuade you. You are capable of accumulating wealth. Your qualities of leadership are obvious; if a tendency to be headstrong is controlled, then you can be a world-beater. When you make up your mind, it is next to impossible for others to persuade you otherwise. Because of this, be sure—and then act. Think and don't merely act for the sake of action.

TAURUS FRIENDS AND PARTNERS

Taurus is harmonious in relation to Pisces, Cancer, Virgo, and Capricorn. With another Taurus, there is a tendency to do much socializing but little work. This is because each is afraid of offending the other; there is instinctive knowledge that two persons determined to have their own way might not have any way. Thus, the fun and games are emphasized, but very little that is of practical value. Taurus is not favorable aspected to Leo, Aquarius, or Scorpio. Taurus can be considered neutral in relation to Aries, Gemini, Libra, and Sagittarius.

TAURUS CAREERS

You like to deal with money; you enjoy being part of a "big deal." You gain pleasure from contemplating the rise of a stock, the rise of an individual from obscurity to prominence. The Tenth House is associated with career;

that sector of your Solar horoscope is Aquarius, giving Uranus as an indicator. You could succeed in areas considered unorthodox, including astrology.

You are a valuable asset to any organization seeking to win friends and influence people. You assume responsibility without becoming unctuous. You do demand authority with responsibility; and you also ask for your fair share of profits. You may not be Einstein, but usually you can do a good job in figuring profit and loss.

You are willing to wait for an opportunity. You make contacts. You build bridges. You are very aware of public relations and could succeed in that field.

Of course, an analysis of your complete horoscope (month, date, year, hour, and place of birth) is required for a definitive statement on occupation. However, with knowledge that your natal Sun is in Taurus, it is possible to gain an overall picture of career indications.

Taurus is the zodiacal sign that is most closely related to money and personal resources, which reveals that you are (more than the average individual) attracted to money and financial activity. You are fascinated with the ups and downs of the stock market. You enjoy giving advice in this area, but often you will reject advice given by an expert. You prefer to make your own money decisions.

You could succeed in a variety of occupations related to money—bank teller, loan officer, business executive, to name but a few in this area. Listen: you could succeed in advertising, publicity, writing, astrological and mathematical research. You are aware of trends, cycles, especially those related to economics. Taureans can find success as singers, beauticians, and in fields where appreciation of beauty adds up to a profitable asset. For Taureans the following occupations are highlighted: artist, musician, singer, actor, florist, women's apparel manufacturer, hotel executive, throat specialist, and photographer.

THE TAURUS HAND

Some astrologers are proficient at guessing Sun signs; that is, they can look at an individual and perceive his, or her, zodiacal sign. This is no easy task—it requires experience, practice. The reason is that the Rising Sign (at the time and place of birth) affects personality and appearance, as does the sign the Moon occupied at birth: yet, the place of the Sun is a strong indicator where character and appearance enter the picture.

Over the years, I have found that one significant key in this effort is the human hand. A person's hand often reveals whether that individual was born under a Fire, Earth, Air, or Water Sign.

Taurus belongs to the Earth element. You are an individual of earthy, basic tastes and this is reflected in the size and shape of your hands. Earth element hands tend to be basic, square-shaped. Your hands are wider than they are long and your thumb can be considered firm to stiff rather than flexible. If you are a negative Taurus—one who cannot control his or her temper—then your thumb is apt to be club-like. In any case, when you attempt to bend back the thumb, it is almost impossible to do so. Lack of flexibility is a definite characteristic. The outstanding characteristic of the Taurus hand is the fact that it is square.

Taurus Secrets

The horoscope, with its twelve angles or Houses, covers every area of life, including your secrets. The Twelfth House holds sway over secret fears, fantasies, undercover problems, all that is hidden or beneath the surface.

In your case, Aries occupies your Twelfth House. The Mars of Aries combines with your Venus significator to show that you are, in secret thoughts, fascinated with the military—extremely pro or against. There is no halfway in this area where you are concerned.

Aries in your Twelfth House also shows that your great fear is lack of security. You are willing to fight for what you think is right; but your weak point is a desire always to be warm and comfortable, to have a roof over your head and to be able to afford it. That seems to be natural, *except* that fearing this lack can become an obsession.

Thus, you collect rather than enjoy money, assets. You build a backlog, saving for a proverbial rainy day. What you must do to overcome secret fear is to perceive that nothing is certain except change. What is today could change tomorrow. In your fantasies, you are debonair, a knight in shining armor, robbing the rich to aid the poor. In actuality, you could become the kind of bargain hunter who substitutes quantity for quality.

All humans fear—it is the *degree* and the area that count. For you, fear can result in haste. Temptation could rear its head—you could take the plunge. You want, bull-like, to rush in where perhaps wiser persons have feared to tread. This does not mean you are wrong—but it could indicate carelessness in sensitive areas.

You fear lack of funds. Usually, you come out on top, smelling like a rose; but statistics don't help here. As each new "emergency" arises, so does the old fear.

You also fear that you will not be loved. This area is of special importance to you. Realizing that this is at the root of many of your anxieties could go a long way in helping you to understand yourself.

Your fears, secrets are linked with domestic harmony, too. You desire a home and a loving mate, preferably one with a melodious voice, one who is the perfect host or hostess. To gain such, you have to cultivate your own tastes—you have to be where the kind of person you seek is likely to be.

Now, what to do about it? First, be willing to take the initiative. You can't do this if you ruminate. You can't always get the answers before viewing the problem. Take a chance on your abilities, on your sense of timing. By getting into action, you actually chase fear. One of your secrets is a strong desire to to be rid of fear. You can start to do so by shaking off lethargy. At least, that's one step.

All of this, as you can see, does require action on your part. You cannot be passive and fulfill secret desires. That, Taurus, should be obvious, You will attract people with money—and the odds are that you will not be short-changed in the financial area. Realize this, *know* it, imprint it in your subconscious. Then there no longer will be any need to entertain *that* secret fear of lack and loss.

Gemini
May 21 - June 20

Birthstone
Pearl

Flower
Rose

Numbers
5, 9, and 3

Color
Yellow

Parts of Body
Hands, Arms, and Lungs

Cities
London, Plymouth, San
Francisco, Melbourne,
Nuremberg, Versailles,
Tripoli

Countries
United States, Belgium,
Wales, West of England,
Lower Egypt, N.E. Coast
of Africa

Your Character and Life

Restless Gemini: the sign which exhibits curiosity, asks questions, moves about, gesticulates—you are the teacher, the social worker, the photographer, the reporter. You "grow" on people; you touch people, you cause them to react. You are vibrant. The opposite sex is drawn to you, although at "crucial" moments you could find something to laugh at—which can be a disconcerting trait.

You are restless and charming. You scatter your forces and some wonder if you ever really do concentrate. You were born under the third zodiacal sign, associated with Mercury; Gemini is an Air Sign, featuring the intellect. You may not be profound, but you are intelligent. You may not be a raving beauty, but you are vivacious. You love change, travel, variety. You can love more than one person at the same time. You often find yourself a puzzle and then wonder why some don't fathom the depths of your character. You are filled with contradictions but are capable of coining up with ready explanations.

You want to be a part of your time, and to help others know *what kind* of time it is.

You are interesting and controversial. Your ideas are not orthodox and neither are your methods. You are versatile, often trying to do too much at once. Many state flatly that you are exasperating.

Gemini is associated with the hands and arms. And your hands are usually busy: pointing, touching, gesturing. An outlet for expression is a definite necessity for you. You are filled with energy and capable of doing almost anything—at a moment's notice. You usually act only according to the way you feel—at the time. Obviously, your character is multifaceted; your emotions run the gamut.

Gemini is the sign of the twins—and *more twins are born from May 21st to June 20th than at any other time of the year.* Gemini, as we say, is associated with the hands. And my own research indicates that *more left-handed people were born under Gemini than under any other sign.*

Gemini is filled with anecdotes; natives of this sign can tell a story at the drop of a hat. Some of their clichés are just as bad as the foregoing, too!

Gemini, being the natural third sign, is associated with short journeys, brothers, sisters, ideas and gossip rather than deep-rooted philosophy. You can do a little of almost everything but what you do best is laugh. Of great value is your ability to laugh at your own foibles.

Gemini is a mutable, airy sign and its chief characteristic is exuberance. Born under Gemini, you equate justice with love.

You have a way, Gemini, of generating enthusiasm. A party seldom remains dull when you're around. People tell anecdotes about you—they gossip with and about you. They are curious about where you've been—and where you're going next. You are so good at commanding attention that you would make an excellent salesperson, as well as a writer, teacher, or reporter—you are on the move, both mentally and physically.

You are filled with qualities of expressiveness. This is fine on the positive side. But, Gemini, once the fine line is passed, the nervous energy becomes mere nervousness. The exuberance becomes a lack of discipline, to the point where you tend to be uncertain, choosing this course, this person—then another, and another. Listen, Gemini: you have to learn what it is you really want, really desire. You are versatile but, unless controlled, the versatility could turn into confusion. You do so many things well . . . but it is difficult for you to concentrate on one project. You think you know what you want—but you also want to try a few more things. Is it any wonder, Gemini, that many of us do find you exasperating? That's true even when we love you—or, perhaps, even more so when we do love you. As a matter of fact, Gemini, you often cause those who love you to suffer because you demand attention—yet, once it is obtained, you lose interest. The grass, when you respond to your negative side, always appears greener elsewhere.

It seems necessary for you to learn by experience. You sometimes have to go through hell to find out how hot it really is down below. You have to be burned before you fear the fire—or respect its power.

Now, let's get to the positive side of your very provocative zodiacal sign . . . which, incidentally, boasts many celebrities, including Judy Garland, Robert Cummings, and Rosalind Russell. On the positive side, you are witty, charming, a brilliant conversationalist. Your mental clarity, your power of reasoning, is something to admire, to envy . . . *when* you respond to your best side. Often you attract the envy of others. And perhaps this accounts for your dual nature. In your life you seem to have more friends when adversity strikes. When you succeed—when you find emotional stability—then, for some odd reason, you attract the envy, the bitterness, the ridicule of others. And, wanting to be wanted, to be admired and loved, you often pull your punches . . . you deliberately fail or trip yourself up emotionally. This is because you sense that when down and out, you will arouse sympathy, even love. So, Gemini, we have a dilemma. When you are crowned by success, there is the twin of jealousy from others. When in trouble, you attract warmth.

Well, we can see you are a complicated and complex individual. You are often not sure of what you want or need, what must be kept and what discarded. You make numerous resolutions only to break them. You make promises to yourself, only to feel guilty because they are not kept. You insist on discovering for yourself the truth or falseness of beliefs. You want to be in the thick of things. You want to be there in person, checking and taking notes—and then letting us in on it through your eyes and emotions. We love you and yet we are puzzled by you. At times, Gemini, I think you expect too much of us—and we expect too much from you.

One of the great astrology teachers and authors—the late Grant Lewi—once said this about you: *It is always with Gemini as he sees it. He will give the other fellow the right to see it differently, without feeling any obligation to agree with him, and he will go his way according to his own bent, with the utmost disregard for differences of opinion.*

I completely agree with Grant Lewi. You are a non-conformist, Gemini. You instigate curiosity and controversy. You debate on the side of unpopular causes and people. You can do so many things that, very often, you are forced to slow down due to nervous exhaustion.

Travel is important for you. You could meet your future mate while on a journey, or a long-distance visit.

Gemini

Your double nature means, Gemini, that you can look one way, and think the other. You can go in one direction, but be headed somewhere else. You can be with one individual and be thinking, feeling, concerned with someone else. Once a relationship is over—for you it is over. The emotions have switched gear—you no longer care to know or be bothered with how your former lover feels or acts. If you are chained down, for one reason or another—when you no longer care but are forced to remain—then pity the person who does the forcing. To put it bluntly, Gemini can be dreadful when chained down.

Listen, Gemini: you are able to read between the lines. When you are right—you are very right. But there are times when you only think, or imagine, there is something to be read between the lines, some hidden meaning. And at those times you are wrong—and very wrong. There is seldom any halfway. With you, Gemini, it is all the way or nothing.

You have wheels turning within—you plan, think, speculate on more than one subject or person at a time. You analyze—want reasons, explanations. You are never satisfied merely that something took place. "Why did it happen?" is your question. Your Solar ruling planet, Mercury, symbolizes thought, communication, journeys, the interrelationship of mind to mind—the desire to know. That's Mercury—and that's you, Gemini. At times you get so filled to the brim with wanting to know that you feel, in reality, there is nothing you really do know. This leads to a lack of security. You become irritable, nervous, careless, exasperated. At these times you seek love—and it could be with the first person who happens along. You grasp opportunity, hold it to you—wring it dry. You don't want to let a real chance slip by, be it in the area of love or professional endeavor.

A key to greater happiness for you is finding an outlet for your intellectual energy. Your needs are not going to be fulfilled by physical love alone. There must be *communication.* There must be challenge . . . challenge to improve yourself, your lover, your situation, condition, appearance. Once the challenge, the outlet, is removed there returns the same old nagging restlessness—the same problems. It is essential that you constantly seek self-improvement, whether it be through the theater, via theatrical productions in which you engage—whether it be through university extension courses or through exciting individuals or books or any other means of improvement or study. You simply cannot sit still mentally. When you do, the steam builds into an emotional explosion.

Gemini, as we say, is associated with the hands and arms and also with the lungs. Gemini persons are nervous, sensitive, drawn to the arts, the creative processes. As a Gemini, you teach, write, report, appear before the public. You are open to various impressions, tend to become dedicated to a person or a task—and you remain so until your interest is suddenly diverted. Then you become just as dedicated to the next project or person.

Many persons think they know the real you. But a survey, Gemini, would very likely show that each person has a different picture, a different description, a different concept of you. And, if the truth be known, you *are* different—according to the occasion, the person, the situation. You are multisided—never the same, always on the go, changing, versatile, and restless. You are not easy to know because, in a way, you are so many persons rolled into one.

Keep yourself busy. Do everything possible to stay active, to continue to learn. Read, write, study, engage in creative hobbies. Finish what you start. Don't leave so many loose ends. Work left unfinished becomes, for you, a jigsaw puzzle. Piecing together the bits becomes almost impossible, causes worry, brooding, depression. And when you find yourself without a program, you begin to get curious about other people. You become, instead of busy, a busybody. You start advising, sermonizing, taking action behind the scenes. This can create resentment, cost you friends, and even leave you open to cruel satire or ridicule.

You have a tendency to *talk* about subjects which interest you. And you find many willing listeners. You could be a success on the lecture platform. You like to write your own lines—and, if an actor, you often try to *rewrite the script*. At times, you talk like an authority without really having a thorough knowledge of your subject. Your enthusiasm gets the best of you. You get carried away. It is important, Gemini, for you to recognize your own limitations. Learn to listen. Learn your lessons. At times, Gemini, you take only a few lessons—and, before we know it, you are attempting to teach the teacher.

You tend to be high-strung, very sensitive. You expect others almost magically to feel that you do know what you're doing. In other words, you expect others to have faith in you. But it is also necessary to win respect, to gain faith, to earn recognition. It is not enough, Gemini, to merely *expect* these things. Don't take persons or situations for granted. Learn to avoid making superficial judgments or actions.

It is not easy for others to know you—it is not easy for you to know yourself. You have been different at different stages of your life; much more so than the average individual.

Avoid dissipating your energies, your time, your emotions; avoid excess in various departments of life. You see, Gemini, you tend to invite trouble through members of the opposite sex. You create the impression of *I don't care.* Nothing, of course, could be further from the truth—because you *do very much care.* And you want others to perceive your sensitiveness. You want others to care to know, to want to understand you. But your actions and statements, at times, cry out in the opposite direction. You become involved. You complicate your relationships. You feel, somehow, everything will be all right in the end—that he, or she, really will understand.

But, Gemini, how about giving us a clue? How about making it easier for all of as to understand—*by understanding yourself?*

Hold fast to your integrity. But do make some concessions to all of us. Slow down so that we have a better chance to *read* you. Once we do know, you can be assured that we do care—and love.

Value yourself, Gemini. Don't give yourself away—not to lovers, not to children, not to job, not to anything. Be of value, not cheap, not something which can be passed on, from hand to hand, job to job, child to child, situation to situation. *Value yourself,* and by so doing, you set in motion dynamic forces which change your life from night to day, from darkness to light—from a sputtering spark to a warm flame, burning with light and love.

Give yourself half a chance, Gemini—and you'll emerge a mature, happy, prosperous individual.

Now, get going—start now!

Attempting to depict your character and life is akin to containing quicksilver. Your planetary significator, Mercury, is symbolic of quickness, change; your mental motor continues to run even when you apparently are at rest. You leave *impressions*. Others don't have an easy time forgetting you; the nuances of your character echo. Some claim you are a mere adventurer; closer to the truth, perhaps, is that you become embroiled in situations, *adventures*. You desire to become *involved*. This latter quality can be endearing. You do not desert in time of adversity. Thus, you are attracted to social work. The poor, the needy can claim your time, thoughts, emotions because you do *become involved*. You see beyond the immediate, although you often act as if you were intent on living from minute to minute. Where Capricorn can be slow, deliberate, where Taurus can ruminate and Sagittarius can philosophize, you can—and usually do—take *immediate* action.

THE GEMINI LOVER

Here are some tips for men about the Gemini woman: you *must* have a sense of humor. Without it, you may as well give up. If you are going to pursue, or be pursued, by a Gemini woman, you simply must know how to laugh. This lady, born under Gemini, is on the go—she wants to know and be seen and she wants to see and ask questions—and to break the bubble of pomposity wherever she finds it. And, men, some times she does talk too much!

If you are not careful, she is liable to grow on you—you acquire a taste for her, just as some people do for lima beans, or buttermilk, or spinach, or grits and eggs. She can be charming, seductive and, on occasion, even reasonable!

Gemini men are versatile, possess plenty of energy and much curiosity about life—and particularly about women. Gemini men expect their women to be cheerful. Gemini men are depressed by depression. Complaining or nagging is one sure way to lose a Gemini man. He can be deceptive in that he probes, trying to find out what you're really made of—testing your sincerity. When forced to face practical issues, the Gemini man can become downcast, bewildered, and give the impression of being hurt.

The Gemini man is elusive, quick with his hands, artistic, restless, with a tendency to try to be everywhere at once. It is best to make him believe that you are many-sided. You see, once he feels he has figured you out—once you are no longer a puzzle or a challenge—the Gemini man is apt to shrug and go on to his next love, his next adventure. He can talk his way into and out of almost anything. Listen to him, but remain skeptical. And keep a Mona Lisa smile on your face. That definitely helps!

The double nature of a Gemini man or woman is something at which to marvel—or to draw back from in fear. It all depends on who's doing the looking—and for what purpose.

YOUR RISING SIGN

All persons born under your sign are not exactly the same, although basic characteristics will hold. A horoscope, in actuality, is a map of the sky based on the time and place of birth. If you are aware of your birth time, here are some variations it may cause in your life and character:

Born between 4:00 and 6:00 A.M., your Rising Sign is apt to be the same as your Sun Sign—Gemini. This emphasizes your mercurial qualities and highlights your restlessness. You are an original thinker, inventive and daring. Often, however, you have so many irons in the fire that your forces are scattered, your concentration diluted, your goals out of focus. You are agile, versatile, witty; your sense of humor is highly developed and you can extricate yourself from the most difficult situations. You should strive to develop a greater degree of patience. Your words come fast—ideas flow. But the key is to penetrate beyond the realm of superficiality. Then you will be making the most of some very fine qualities.

Born between 6:00 and 8:00 A.M., your Ascendant is probably Cancer, associated with the Moon. This combines with your Mercury to make you more practical than the average native of Gemini. You are drawn to the world of finance. You learn the value of money. You are creative and more likely to stick with a project than the classic native of your sign. You are sensitive, moody, but confident that "time will tell," that your ideas and efforts will be vindicated. You are an innovator and, if you have Cancer rising, your home could be unique—perhaps not ornate, not a showplace in the standard sense, but certainly comfortable, fun, and a place where interesting people gather to express views.

Born between 8:00 and 10:00 A.M., your Rising Sign is likely to be Leo, ruled by the Sun. This combines with your Mercury to provide more warmth than is expressed by the classic Gemini. This means that you are romantic, affectionate, and more apt to be constant in affairs of the heart. You do exhibit a tendency to seek perfection; in this sense, you are more a *romanticist* than you are romantic. You create—and you want to dominate. You want to shape people, places, events. You want to *influence.* You are dramatic—you can sell ideas. Often you are more capable of putting across an idea than following it through to completion. Your personality is dynamic, compelling; people know you're around and you are likely to make an indelible mark. You have *style.* You are unique. You are an original!

Born between 10:00 a.m. and 12:00 noon, your Ascendant is likely to be Virgo, associated with Mercury. That planet is also your Sun Sign significator; the "double dose" of Mercury indicates varied interests. You are versatile; you reach far—you're never satisfied to sit still, never satisfied with the status quo. Your outstanding quality is a sense of humor. You are analytical, discriminating, capable of discerning *reasons.* You seldom are satisfied to know merely that something occurred; you want to know why it happened. You could write, report, collect data; you would be a good detective because you are fascinated with clues. You are restless, fond of travel—your energy seems boundless. But you do require rest, sleep, proper diet—more so than does the average individual.

Born between 12:00 noon and 2:00 P.M., your Rising Sign is apt to be Libra, ruled by Venus. This, combined with your Mercury, highlights mental faculties, especially intuition. Where some deduct and analyze, your strong point is perception. You perceive trends, cycles. Some consider you lucky. It is more than that; it is *timing.* When you follow through on a hunch, you are at the right place at the proper time. Education means much to you—not only for yourself, but for those you consider underprivileged. Your sense of justice is sharply honed. You can see through a phony. You are more patient than is the average member of your sign. But once you get the facts, nothing can stop you from acting to secure justice.

Born between 2:00 and 4:00 P.M., your Ascendant is likely to be Scorpio, with Pluto as significator. This, combined with your Mercury Solar ruler gives you a broad view. Some say you are too broad-minded; your views are futuristic, liberal. Many, who feet oppressed, confide. You are the *last* to cast stones. Your sexual attitudes are liberal; you believe that what occurs in private between two consenting adults is none of your, or anyone else's business. You are attractive; very often, however, you draw to you persons who draw no response from you. Which means that you are selective; you, unlike many natives of your sign, are the opposite of superficial. You look beyond the surface for lasting values.

Gemini

Born between 4:00 and 6:00 P.M., your Rising Sign is apt to be Sagittarius, associated with Jupiter. This, combined with your Mercury significator, gives you the impetus to observe and write, to travel and create, to advocate the open road and open mind. You can handle responsibility more adequately than can the average native of your sign. You are cheerful, optimistic, but you must have a *purpose.* You are not satisfied to wander aimlessly; you are the reformer, the individual with a marked social conscience. You are attracted to educational pursuits, to law—and are intrigued with the history of religion, You have a knack, too, of getting paid for what interests you. You are a practical idealist.

Born between 6:00 and 8:00 P.M., your Ascendant is probably Capricorn, ruled by Saturn. This, combined with your Mercury, causes you to be more reflective than the average person born under your sign. The humor is there, but not so quick to bubble to the surface. You are capable of handling details, but also able to see a project as a whole. You have executive qualities—you would make an excellent assignment editor. Your desire for accuracy is almost a fetish; you research, you use the dictionary, you store facts and utilize them. You expect no less of others, causing some to think of you as a stern taskmaster. Your attitudes are definite, strong. You seldom say one thing and mean another. You are more reserved than the classic native of your sign. You are capable of piecing together bits of information and coming up with the complete story.

Born between 8:00 and 10:00 P.M., your Rising Sign is likely to be Aquarius, ruled by Uranus. This combines with your Mercury to make you even more unorthodox than the average native of your sign. You aim for the future to such an extent that you often neglect the present. In short, you are a visionary. You are concerned with aviation, space, television. Medicine, too, intrigues you, but your ideas are advanced and don't always meet with immediate acceptance. On a positive level, you are brilliant. On the negative side, you could be a victim of self-deception. You break rules but, in most cases, you have also taken the time to become thoroughly familiar with them. You are stubborn when you believe in a cause—you can be a crusader who wins against the odds.

Born between 10:00 P.M., and 12:00 midnight, your Rising Sign is likely to be Pisces, giving you Neptune as the ruling planet. This, combined with your Mercury Solar significator, makes you capable of handling more than one project at a time. Your intuitive intellect provides quick answers; you *know* what must be done—and when. You are versatile, sensitive, aware. At times, you neglect details. You are anxious to perceive entire meanings—in doing so, some of the essentials fall by the wayside. You are poetic, artistic; there is an air of illusion, of mystery about you. Many confide secrets because they sense you already know them. Some claim you are psychic. It is true that you often come up with answers *before* the question is asked. You desire facts, but often cannot provide rational explanations for your opinions. You are more likely to be subjective than objective.

Gemini

Born between 12:00 midnight and 2:00 A.M., your Rising Sign is apt to be Aries, ruled by Mars. This combines with your Mercury to give you an active, inquiring mind. You have more persistence than does the average native of your sign. You are also apt to be more pugnacious; you don't mind a good fight. It clears the air. You are a pioneer, often stepping into situations which others are too conservative to touch. Original ideas are almost second nature; you invent, originate, innovate. When you're around, most persons know it. You assert yourself. You are a reformer who is willing to set an example. You seldom ask others to do what you would not endure. You are impulsive, often headstrong. Your personality and emotions are well-integrated; you have a great degree of self-familiarity. This means you know what you need and how to get it.

Born between 2:00 and 4:00 A.M., your Ascendant is likely to be Taurus, ruled by Venus. This combines with your Mercury Solar ruler to give you an appreciation for beauty, art, music. You are, unlike many born under your sign, also capable of handling money. You know the value of objects of art; you can sense talent, collect and represent it. You have good judgment when it comes to collecting and to investing—from art to real estate. You don't always know why you decide one way or another—but you *feel* what is right. You possess great powers of persuasion. You gain through diplomacy rather than force; the soft sell wins for you. You may not be as agile as the typical native of your sign, but your pace is steady. You are usually there at the finish of a contest.

Gemini Friends and Partners

Gemini is harmonious in relation to Aries, Leo, Libra, and Aquarius. With another Gemini, there is action. You begin projects. You renovate and revise; you modernize. The relationship is stimulating. Ideas are transformed into action. With another Gemini, there are inventions, pioneering projects. Impulse rules and the pace is quick. Gemini is not favorably aspected to Virgo or Pisces—the sign is in opposition to Sagittarius, and generally neutral to Taurus, Cancer, Scorpio, and Capricorn.

Gemini Careers

Your Tenth House, that section of the chart associated with career, is Pisces. The Neptune of Pisces, blended with your Mercury Solar ruler, indicates that you could excel in a field that demands versatility, imagination, creative ability. You could represent a special group, club, organization. You do well in public relations; you would make a fine cruise host or hostess. You can bring people together, help them to enjoy themselves. You might enable people to get together in a special-interest enterprise such as a trip, a stock-purchasing group or club.

You work well behind the scenes. You can keep a secret, despite the fact that you talk a great deal. You are, of course, a natural teacher, reporter, photographer. You would do well in such an organization as a hospital, especially as an X-ray technician.

You need a certain amount of freedom of thought and expression. You can reveal your own personal secrets but can be close-mouthed where the welfare of an organization is concerned.

You know how to laugh in the face of apparent adversity. You can be counted on to find something amusing about almost anything—especially emergencies.

Because of your love of movement, you should succeed in occupations connected with transportation. Detail work upsets you. Your enthusiasm is catching—and, thus, as a teacher you would inspire your students. Other occupations connected with Gemini include: writer, orator, graphologist, dietitian, detective, editor, actor, radio or television announcer.

Your wit is sharp; you could make good as a newspaper feature writer, or as a comedian.

Red tape, drudgery upset you. It would be better to leave details to others. Your sense of humor and nose for news dominate: you gain and impart knowledge and, as a publicity director, would plant stories that got printed and utilize radio and television.

You are in the thick of current events—travel, news, "happenings." You can dig in, go after a story and track it down. You don't know the meaning of the word "quit."

If you control impulse, permit logic to have a say, learn the virtue of patience—you can be successful.

THE GEMINI HAND

Some astrologers are proficient at guessing Sun signs; that is, they can look at an individual and perceive his, or her, zodiacal sign. This is no easy task—it requires experience, practice. The reason is that the Rising Sign (at the time and place of birth) affects personality and appearance, as does the sign the Moon occupied at birth. Yet, the place of the Sun is a strong indicator where character and appearance enter the picture.

Over the years, I have found that one significant key in this effort is the human hand. A person's hand often reveals whether that individual was born under a Fire, Earth, Air, or Water Sign.

You, Gemini, were born under an Air Sign; Gemini belongs to the Air element. The Air Trinity represents the triangular hand. You can recognize it because it is the opposite of the Earth type. The Earth type is square, basic. Your hand, Gemini, is angular, a triangle, it tapers toward the fingers: is not basic, but is sensitive, expressive. You use your hands to gesticulate, to illustrate, to point, not only outward, but to yourself, often in a comical way, at times in a very "sexy" way. Beautiful Gemini women can devastate one by blithely pointing, in an unconscious manner, toward themselves. Sort of like saying, "Take me!" The Gemini hand is usually long and thin, with more lines on the palm than are to be found in the other groups. The Air Trinity people are intellectual; they can capture the pulse of the public. They set the pace and are busy, busy. This is quite an easy hand to recognize.

GEMINI SECRETS

The horoscope, with its twelve angles or Houses, covers every area of life, including your secrets. The Twelfth House holds sway over secret fears, fantasies, undercover problems, all that is hidden or beneath the surface.

In your case, Taurus occupies your Twelfth House. The Venus of Taurus combines with your Mercury significator to stress intuition, appreciation of beauty, art. It makes you extremely sensitive to the thoughts, feelings, moods, intentions of others.

One of your major secrets is a desire to be an object of sexual admiration. In actuality, your sense of humor often "interferes" with any *femme fatale* impression. But in your fantasies (man or woman) you are languorous; you exude sex and, instead of being your actual quick, flighty self, are slow, rhythmic, and sensual in your movements.

Although, in actuality, you may appear to have a devil-may-care attitude, your secret self is concerned with possessions, security, money. Perhaps that is part of your apparent double nature; this sharp line between what you *appear* to be and what your secret visions entail.

Another of your secrets is contained in the area of travel. You fantasize in this manner, perhaps; you see yourself hurtling through space, breaking speed and distance records. You are acclaimed for your journey into space. You find this invigorating; it stimulates you and you are reluctant to "return to Earth."

The "flight through space" syndrome does contain sexual connotations. Because you belong to the intellectual Air element, it is natural for you to desire acclaim secretly. But the acclaim, within your secret self, comes in a combination of Venus (the physical) and Mercury (the mental). Thus, the space travel (sophisticated, intellectual achievement) and the speed (sex) blend.

One of your fears is a "lack." Lack of goods, lack of sex appeal, lack of what you require to put across thoughts, ideas, lack of communication. You also secretly fear being restricted, tied down, confined. You tend to fear the formal, including clothes that choke or restrict. You want to share knowledge, but fear some of your ideas may not rest on a sound philosophical base.

Of course, Gemini, you must realize that these secret apprehensions may not *themselves* contain a solid foundation. Accept them as fantasies. Learn from them, but don't be *dominated* by them.

You are outgoing, friendly, demonstrative. And, whether or not you are aware of it, you possess plenty of sex appeal!

Listen: get yourself a hidden reserve of cash. The actual amount doesn't make much difference. Just know it is there— that's what counts. This will help relieve some of your insecurity. You fear (one of your secrets) being "caught short." Save up some "mad money."

Your subconscious tends to be fixed, stubborn, unlike your personality, which is flexible. Again, that dual nature! Build hidden resources. Then, as if by magic, much emotional doubt will vanish: you'll feel more adequate and, thus, you will *be* more adequate.

If the truth be known, Gemini, you are capable of being heroic, intellectual, physically attractive; you can be a heroic lover, with cash in the bank, and a dashing air. Imprint this on your subconscious.

Then, Gemini, one of your secrets will be confidence!

Cancer

June 21 - July 22

Birthstone
Moonstone

Flower
Larkspur

Numbers
2, 7, and 3

Color
Violet

Part of Body
Breasts and Stomach

Cities
New York, Tunis, Algiers,
Amsterdam, Constantino-
ple, Venice, Genoa, Milan,
Manchester, Stockholm

Countries
North and West Africa, Isle
of Mauritius, Paraguay,
Scotland, Holland

YOUR CHARACTER AND LIFE

Your memories are of family and you do a lot of talking about family ties; any revelation about you would have to concern your thoughts about parents and children. Family represents security, stability to you; that is where your interests lie. It is to the area of security that you gravitate. Words such as protection, shelter, and food represent symbols with which you are familiar. On the positive side, you acquire—you utilize skills to attain stature and to obtain necessities. You can also become wealthy, as witness the fact that many persons successful in commerce and industry were born under Cancer. On the negative side, you are possessive. You want to "hang on" to persons and possessions. Cancer is associated with the Moon; if anyone can be moody, it is you. You change moods as often as some people do handkerchiefs or socks. But perhaps, Cancer, I should say you are sensitive to moods around you; you are impressionable and your own feelings are subject to atmosphere, aura, family harmony, or lack of it.

Your subconscious is steeped in tradition, community, customs, habits. Once patterns are established, they take root as far as you are concerned. Yours is the natural fourth zodiacal sign; it relates to land, a place to anchor, a harbor in a storm. You are loyal to family, country; but in affairs of the heart you are intense and do not feel that you must necessarily be "chained down" to a member of the opposite sex.

Your intensity is of the kind that enables you to tear down in order to rebuild. If your heart's desire will not conform to your desires, you do not hesitate to try some revamping.

You put on the pressure. If this does no good, then you will find it perfectly logical to conclude the relationship. Your ideal in an affair of the heart is the eventual establishment of a home, a castle—an empire. You acquire goods. If your partner or would-be mate will not fit into this mold, then you lose a vital spark, the fire of interest. The magnetism weakens, fades, and the attraction dissolves. *That's one of many major revelations about you, Cancer.*

Your sign belongs to the Water element, is the natural fourth sign—said to be governed by the Moon—and your need to feel secure is almost legendary among astrologers. You can brood and worry, you can imagine, you can take on the ailments of others—you can be so receptive that you begin to take on the "coloring" of others. You perceive. You are prescient. Your sensitivity enables you to know, in advance, what another person is thinking. You anticipate the actions of others. Thus, Cancer, it is not surprising that you can be one step ahead, especially where business affairs are concerned.

You are solid and weak. You are a contradiction because, like your Moon symbol, you are subject to change—without notice. Yet, you have a keen sense of responsibility. You are aware of the past as well as the present. And, Cancer, you constantly strive to perceive future trends and cycles—especially where real estate enters the picture— knowing the *future* values of land and property. At times, it could truly be said you are "in the thick of the future."

Family and home play a paramount role in your life. Family can bring either great happiness or be the cause of depression. If you are to be strong, you must master emotions, or at least bring them under reasonable control.

You are imaginative, romantic, sentimental. You tend to become *attached* to the lives of others; you can "lose" yourself in the emotions, actions, reactions of other people. You are, at times, capable of observing a stranger and experiencing his emotions, feelings, the events in his life—at times, even his future. That's where your ESP comes into play.

However, the key is to live a life of your own. Learn to "let go." Don't hang on to children, possessions, outmoded ideas and methods. Get your sense of loyalty into the proper perspective. Don't think you have to sacrifice without asking, thinking, reasoning, probing. Be warm and sensitive and loyal—but not self-sacrificing to the degree that you make yourself a welcome mat to anyone who wants to rub his feet and walk in, uninvited.

As is certainly true of us all, Cancer, there are contradictions to your makeup. For example: you are practical, yet soft to the point of sogginess. You are strong, yet weak to the point of giving until you can't give anymore. You insist, only to give in; you are perceptive, but you can walk into trouble with your eyes wide open.

Obviously, it is important that you learn to distinguish between generosity and foolishness. And stop trying to guide, influence, sway the lives of others. Don't deceive yourself by saying you are only doing what's best for those close to you. Very often, this means, Cancer, that you are only acting on your own behalf, giving in to your own whims, desires, and fears.

Check yourself when you begin to nag. Accept the fact that there is a shade of gray, not just black and white, good and bad, poor and rich. Lose an argument and yet appreciate the excitement of intellectual exchange. It is not always necessary to "win" in order to gain valuable information.

You are warm, at times sensuous, even generous. But when you are these things—when you are giving and warm—the terms are apt to be your own. It is not easy for you to *give* in the sense of giving up a point, giving in, giving to the point of relinquishing something dear to you, be it in actual object or an idea. It seems, Cancer, that very often the emphasis is *on your terms.* And because of this, many tend to cater to you. However, you do not necessarily appreciate this—you don't want to be catered to—you want to be respected. Learn to utilize power intelligently. Adapt yourself to power. Learn to handle authority. Overcome any tendency to be "bossy." Many times, you *assume* the role of a father or mother: you direct instead of persuade, you insist instead of reasoning, you demand instead of asking.

The late, great American astrologer, Evangeline Adams, claimed that the classic, or typical, Cancer—after years of struggling with the wanderlust—comes back to the place of birth. It is there, Cancer, that you are happiest—at home, your birthplace, for you never lose that loyalty to home, family, community, country. This holds despite the fact that the Moon significator is one of change, drawing you to the sea, instilling in you a desire to travel, even while purchasing land for its future value, even while building a home, even while planning to "settle down."

Your personal desire is to earn respect. And this you can do through your many fine, sensitive qualities. You must also control a tendency to dominate by power, force, shouting—or, at the opposite end of the pole, in a kind of reverse twist, by being quietly dramatic and appealing to a so-called sense of duty. Obviously, Cancer, you often get what you *apparently* want. But what you really *need* is often another story. To get what you need, you have to throw aside crutches and gimmicks. You have to be forthright, frank, thorough.

You are not easy to analyze. One part of you is practical. Another is moody, changeable, romantic. If these ingredients could be blended in a balanced manner, you would be on top, unbeatable. And, most important, you would be happy.

You do have a definite knack for sensing what people are feeling, thinking. You have what might be termed *emotional insight*. You have a built-in lie detector; you can tell the difference between sincerity and sham. You can detect the difference, also, between mere boasting and actual ability. You *know* what is superficial and what actually contains substance. But what you do with this special insight is the question—something you have to answer for, and to yourself. This "extra information" can actually be a disadvantage. It places added responsibility on your shoulders. The responsibility results in either strength—or panic. That's why perhaps, you are subject to so many moods: you can be amiable, giving, one minute, and ready to fight and be stubborn the next moment. You are a paradox, not only to yourself, but to others—especially family members.

You are very protective, willing to sacrifice for your family, loved ones. But in so doing, you often arouse animosity. I repeat it because it is a sort of paradox. It doesn't sound fair . . . or even logical. But I find that it is true. It has much to do with human nature. You see, Cancer, when you sacrifice, you put others in your debt—and no matter how close they are to you, there seems bound to be some kind of resentment, some kind of animosity, some subtle overtone of friction. Now, the lesson you learn is this: help others to help themselves. But, Cancer, don't interfere, don't become the director . . . don't try to dominate with an attitude of *I know what's best and we'll do it my way.*

Cancer, as we say, is associated with the Moon, and your sign is related to the chest, the breasts, the stomach. Cancer belongs to the Water Trinity, and is the zodiacal sign of someone who is emotional, sensitive, moody, has a love of security, and appreciates the past as well as the present. Evangeline Adams once said of your sign: *a love of antiquity and of old, established things often manifests itself in the native, and he may take a deep interest in old books, paintings, bric-a-brac, or in some such half-forgotten science as heraldry. The energetic type,* Miss Adams went on to say, *occupies itself more exclusively with the affairs of the moment, and is apt to have a contempt for anything that is not entirely up to date.*

It would appear that Miss Adams detected the numerous contradictions in your nature, as I do. She said that although your sign is symbolized by the Crab—and is of the Water element—that did not mean there was anything wishy-washy about you. She said that one quality, more than any other, stands out for you: that is *tenacity.* I agree. You hold on to things, situations, persons. That's why so many Cancer people are listed in *Who's Who in Commerce and Industry* . . . because you also know how to hold on to money. And you hold on to your past. No matter how far you travel, you tend to return to the place where you were born. Your birthplace, your home—these are basic qualities you can understand. You can be loyal to your country, your community.

Food is basic and, as we say, Cancer rules the stomach. This has a bearing on your outlook. Cities have horoscopes . . . were "born" under zodiacal signs. Paris is Leo—and New York City is Cancer. That's why there are more restaurants in New York than any other city in the world. People in New York become part of the rhythm of the Cancer city and become conscious of dining out.

To get back to Evangeline Adams, who was such a delightful woman and a credit to astrology. She said that Cancer newlyweds often spend so much money on their dining-room furniture that they have nothing left with which to furnish the rest of the house. That's Cancer! The rest of the house can be empty . . . *but there is going to be a place to eat!* Cancers sometimes become so interested in the family kitchen that they get in each other's way. On the positive side, however, they are wonderful chefs and a delight—when they don't make too much of a good thing. It is strange that Cancer people do have a tendency to exaggerate the importance that eating plays in the scheme of human welfare, of happiness, of contentment. I am going to repeat a warning that Evangeline Adams once gave to the Cancer-born. She said: *Cancer people should always recognize the fact that drinking as well as eating may become a menace to their health and to their success.* The lesson here, Cancer, is simple . . . Miss Adams was urging you to practice moderation. Don't overdo. Curb your tendency to make something big out of nothing, which means not only to curb your tendency to go to extremes in eating and drinking, but to restrain your emotions when you find yourself going overboard.

What I want to say is this: although you love your family . . . although you mean well . . . you must loosen the reins. You must not interpret a desire for freedom on the part of others as a rebuff to you. *You don't own anyone.* Eventually each person must be their own person . . . must be true to the self. This need not mean the individual has less love for you. But each person, Cancer, must also have a certain amount of *self-love* . . . and respect.

Listen, Cancer: you feel you know what is right or wrong and so why should there be any question, any debate. And, as a matter of fact, you *are* a wonderful counselor . . . you do have a talent for guiding people, steering them in the right direction. You have a way of influencing people even though they may not entirely agree with you. But, still, you must grant others their freedom of choice.

Many celebrities were born under Cancer, including Jane Russell, John Glenn, Marc Chagall, and chef Mike Roy, with whom I authored a book, *Cooking with Astrology* (Llewellyn Publications, St. Paul, 1998).

I have said that you can be possessive . . . that you hold on to persons, that you are loyal and stick to a project until it is completed . . . whether that project be the building of a home or a career. You have a hunger for security—for permanence. You want stability, understanding, harmony, a method—a rhyme and a reason. But what you *want*, Cancer, and what you *find* are often two different things. And so when you do find what you are looking for, know it and stick to it. But, on the other side of the coin, also know when you have not found what is desired. Don't stick to something merely out of a kind of misguided loyalty. Learn to recognize a lost cause . . . and be willing to give it up. If you learn this, you will have achieved one of the secrets of attaining personal fulfillment. And I repeat—know when you are involved in a lost cause, and drop it before you become resigned to frustration, ill-health, disappointment, puzzlement, bitterness. Be loyal and stick to persons, situations who *deserve* it. But *know* when you simply have run up against the wrong person or situation—wrong for you—and bow out. This, Cancer, will save you much emotional wear and tear. It's important that you absorb this bit for information—for, left to your own devices, you can be like a horse in a burning barn—you're tenacious and simply will refuse to budge. *I want you to budge, to move, when move you must.*

You are perceptive . . . it is not really easy to fool you. But you are good at *fooling yourself.* You can put on a pair of rose-colored glasses . . . and peer through them when all the time you actually are aware that the picture is not rosy.

Some of your hopes and wishes tend to be impractical. You know the facts but, at times, you find it difficult to separate facts from desires. When the mood strikes you, you can be extravagant. You see, Cancer, you are fond of comfort, and once you cross the line, the fondness for comfort, for security, turns into a demand for luxury. When this happens, you waste time, emotions, and money.

My friend and colleague, the brilliant astrologer Carl Payne Tobey, claims that Cancer is always somewhat the baby whose feelings are easily hurt. Tobey says the Cancer woman expects parents, and all men to treat her like a baby. But Tobey points out that she isn't a baby when it comes to being able to take care of herself. She capitalizes on her ability to make other people take care of her. Meanwhile, claims astrologer Tobey, the Cancer woman will be secretly hiding her money and setting it aside for a rainy day. If her husband goes broke, he will suddenly get a surprise. His Cancer wife will come to the rescue. Finally, Tobey's research indicates that Cancer women can read and understand men like a book.

You don't "laugh" Cancer people out of anything. The emotions of Cancer must be handled with kid gloves. Otherwise, emotional wounds occur, and they are slow to heal. Those born under your sign, Cancer, are more sensitive than might be imagined. Although you can be practical about ordering a meal, about making restaurant reservations, about judging the value of property—you are anything but practical where emotions are concerned. To put it another way: you are "touchy." Good humor will work with Gemini and some of the other signs. But Cancer takes itself seriously. So much so that, once a project is begun, the path is followed to completion. Being of a Cardinal sign, you have a sense of destiny: you feel, in effect, that if you are doing something it is important. It is important because *you* are involved. You wouldn't be interested if it wasn't something of consequence. Thus, in dealing with Cancer, one doesn't ridicule a proposition; one attempts to reason, one can do a reverse twist by asking questions . . . hoping that Cancer, through his answers, will reveal to himself the truth of the matter.

Encouragement and praise do wonders for you. Thus, it is important that your friends are persons who do not "pull you down." This is not to say you should surround yourself with an army of "yes men." But it is to indicate the importance of being with jovial persons who, when they do criticize, do so in a mature manner, aimed at building rather than tearing down.

You are a sensitive individual, more emotional than the average; your makeup is one of contradictions. You will protect what is your own, but you will give up much for the sake of family. You want security, yet feel a constant need for change, experiment, probing action.

The Cancer woman desires the best for her children Thus, despite her need for a secure feeling, she is willing to take risks, to give up much, so that her family can have social as well as financial advantages.

THE CANCER LOVER

Now, here are some special hints for men about Cancer women: they are lovely and often lonely—they reach out for love and affection. Often, when their desires for security are not fulfilled, they stray. They seek—they give in to curiosity, longing. But once the Cancer woman is given love, she is faithful, loyal, warm, and exciting. And as I have said, she can also cook!

Here are some tips for women about the Cancer man: be sympathetic to his needs, his aspirations, but don't spoil him. He is emotional, sensitive to his surroundings, and to your moods. And he has no shortage of moods himself. Cancer men appreciate the home and good food. But, even more so, the Cancer man appreciates *homemaking efforts*, including the talents that make a skilled chef. He does not require a palace or a queen, but he does insist on undivided loyalty. He is an idealist and not the easiest man to please. You see, the Cancer man expects to make mistakes, but he is *astonished* when a loved one slips in any manner. This man actually enjoys a good family quarrel. Seems to feel it clears the air! But let an outsider say something about a person he loves—that's a different story.

YOUR RISING SIGN

All persons born under your sign are not exactly the same, although basic characteristics will hold. A horoscope, in actuality, is a map of the sky based on time and place of birth. One of the most important parts of the horoscope is the Rising Sign, which is the sign coming up over the eastern horizon when you were born. If you are aware of your birth time, note these variations of life and character within the Cancer sign:

Born between 4:00 and 6:00 A.M., the Cancer qualities are intensified, because it is likely that your Rising Sign is Cancer. You also have the Sun in that zodiacal sign. Thus the Moon influence is doubled. You are intense in that part of your nature related to love. You can be overly possessive. You are loyal, but also vulnerable. You pay too much attention to rumors. People report to you on clandestine affairs. You take too seriously mere hearsay. For your own peace of mind, it is necessary that you differentiate between fact and rumor. Otherwise, you become one who is a victim of a persecution complex. You become, in your our own mind, a martyr. On the positive side, you may experience something that is akin to a cornucopia of plenty.

Born between 6:00 and 8:00 A.M., it is likely that Leo is your Rising Sign or Ascendant. Dignity, showmanship, a sense of drama can be added to your Cancer characteristics. Leo is associated with the Sun; this, combined with the Moon as your Cancer significator, makes you more extravagant, gives you a greater love of luxury and adds to the sensuousness of your nature. You attract young persons—your sense of humor is more pronounced. When you dine, it is apt to be a production. When you present someone with a gift, it is apt to be on a grand scale. Your home could be a showplace. Whatever you do must reflect your personality. What you own mirrors your style, carrying the "vibration" of your personal charisma.

Born between 8:00 and 10:00 A.M., your Ascendant is likely to be Virgo. This brings Mercury into combination with your Moon—makes you more analytical than is the average Cancer individual. You are thrifty because you have learned the value of money. You seek perfection and this often leads to disappointment. You can spot a phony a mile away; it isn't easy to fool you. But you often make excuses for those who attract you. That's why it is not unlikely that you deceive yourself about the opposite sex. You desire order; you can be precise. But you can also break the rules once they are mastered. This is a good combination—Cancer Sun and Virgo Ascendant—it adds up to perception, intelligence. You are your own worst critic. Start liking yourself more—then others will follow suit.

Born between 10:00 A.M. and 12:00 noon, your Rising Sign is likely to be Libra, adding to your sensitivity and sense of good living. You appreciate beauty; you probably have innate talent as a designer. You also have a sense of rhythm which could express itself in music or writing. The Venus of Libra combines with your Moon significator to make you a creative individual, with unique tastes and a distinct style. Your intuitive qualities are accented; you have a greater sense of justice than does the average individual born under Cancer. You are attractive to the opposite sex; you have a natural beauty which is captivating. If a man, you exude a kind of personal magnetism which women find hard to resist.

Born between 12:00 noon and 2:00 P.M., your Rising Sign is likely to be Scorpio, associated with the planet Pluto. Your desire to love is highly developed. You can be more intense than the average individual born under Cancer. You are possessive; your creative urges are powerful. It is all the way or nothing; there is very little in between or halfway where you are concerned. It is necessary for you to feel wanted, loved; you need to "belong." Your ideals, where love enters the picture, are high. Because of this, disappointment is no stranger to you. When involved with someone, you demand all of that individual. Anyone who holds back, who is lukewarm, is not for you.

Born between 2:00 and 4:00 P.M., your Rising Sign is likely to be Sagittarius. The Jupiter significator of this sign combines with your Moon Solar ruler to make you inquisitive, idealistic; it intensifies your desire to travel, to know, to publish, to be a part of your time. You would make a fine administrator; you are especially capable of detecting trends and this could be applied to the stock market. This period is very good, also, for writing, publishing, and advertising. You are more expansive than is the average person born under your sign. Your appeal is to large groups rather than to individuals. A career on the stage is not unlikely; you are capable of transmitting emotions across the footlights.

Born between 4:00 and 6:00 P.M., your Ascendant is likely to be Capricorn, bringing Saturn into play with your Moon Sun sign ruler. You are apt to be more reserved than is the average Cancer person. Also, you are more patient, regarding *time* as an ally. You are conscious of security and aware of the necessity of a "good" marriage. With this in your consciousness, you take pains to choose, to compare, to wait and observe, until you are positive that a life partner is suited to your requirements. Although you give a conservative appearance, you are willing to back up convictions with action. You are stronger willed than is the average Cancerian. You are conscientious and attract people to you with their problems—and their money.

Born between 6:00 and 8:00 P.M., your Rising Sign is likely to be Aquarius; the planetary significator is Uranus. This makes you more inquisitive than is the average individual born under Cancer. Uranus combined with your Moon Solar ruler makes a formidable team. You are not only aware of security, but also concerned with the future. Your home is apt to be modernistic; your views run along unorthodox lines. Your attitude is one of live and let live. Your circle of friends is wide; you are attractive, stubborn at times, yet a streak of amiability draws praise from persons in various walks of life. For you, no desire is really out of reach. You perceive ways and means of accomplishing faraway goals. You are more social than is the classic Cancer.

Born between 8:00 and 10:00 P.M., your Rising Sign is likely to be Pisces, giving you Neptune as ruler of the Ascendant. This, combined with the Moon, heightens your sensitivity, makes you subject to various moods and draws you to the sea. It is necessary for you to be aware of liquid intake; your "thirst," at times, could exceed limits of moderation. Many claim you are psychic. You work well as a director of an institution, such as a hospital. You can function alone better than can most persons. There is an air of mystery about you which intrigues. This quality could make you a "box office" attraction; people are interested, curious about what you do, think, and say.

Born between 10:00 P.M. and 12:00 midnight, your Rising Sign is likely to be Aries, bringing Mars into play with your Moon Solar ruler. You are more aggressive than the average Cancer. You are dynamic, an individual who prefers actions to words. Very often, impulse tends to dominate logic with you. You tend to be ahead of your time; thus, it is important that you learn lessons of restraint. You possess social zeal; you are a reformer. You battle for what you believe to be right. However, your timing is not always the best; you anticipate what *could* be, but you can be premature. Self-control could make your life a happier one, especially in the domestic area—an area of paramount importance to you. Obviously, you prefer taking the lead; following others is not your cup of tea.

Born between 12:00 midnight and 2:00 A.M., your Ascendant is likely to be Taurus, a sign ruled by Venus. This, combined with your Moon, makes you sensuous. You appreciate beauty, comfort, especially in home surroundings.

You know the value of money and are not apt to squander it. You are an excellent financial adviser; you can spot bargains and obtain them. You accumulate; you build files. You can be devastating to one who challenges your ability or knowledge. But, for a friend, you build assets—and a great defense against adversaries. Where love is concerned, you are discriminating. But your emotions often dominate logic; you tend to draw to you persons who are less than worthy. Be more selective; listen to your head as well as your heart.

Born between 2:00 and 4:00 A.M., your Rising Sign is likely to be Gemini, associated with Mercury. This combination—Gemini Ascendant and Cancer Sun sign—creates a desire to "touch" life. You do things with your hands. You are nimble, perceptive, versatile. You can be impatient, quick; your mental processes are agile. You have a desire to correct flaws; at times, this can be tiresome. Others often find it difficult to keep up with you. The pace you set is fast. You are analytical, flexible, capable of adjusting to changing conditions and times. Control your moods and you control your destiny. Stick with a project; then success will not merely be a flirtation—it can be something permanent.

CANCER FRIENDS AND PARTNERS

Cancer is harmonious in relation to Taurus, Virgo, Scorpio, and Pisces. With another Cancer, the association tends to get tied down with red tape. It is not the most exciting relationship. Two Cancer individuals are apt to find much to criticize about each other. Your sign is not favorably aspected to Aries, Libra, or Capricorn. Cancer can be considered neutral where the following signs are concerned: Leo, Sagittarius, Aquarius, and Gemini.

CANCER CAREERS

You are much aware of career—and security. You ruminate about your vocation; your view is toward the future, although you are sentimental about the past.

It's important that you do not fall into a pattern or rut from which it is difficult to move, express yourself or change. You can, if not wary, become a creature of habit.

The Tenth House is associated with career; that sector of your Solar horoscope contains Aries, giving Mars as the significator. You should be active, not passive, where your career is concerned. This sector is also associated with ambition, prestige, standing in the community.

You learn by teaching; by sharing knowledge you build up a reservoir of goodwill. You are intuitive about business, career, ambitions. You know what should be done; it is a matter of *doing* it.

Of course, an analysis of your complete horoscope (month, date, year, hour, and place of birth) is required for a definitive statement on occupation. However, with the knowledge that your natal Sun was in Cancer, it is possible to gain an overall picture of career indications.

Generally, you should be in a position where you are free to take action. You can perceive the needs of the public. Often, this perception takes the form of prescience; you can be ahead of the crowd, of the current trend, of associates. If you are held back by lack of authority, much impetus is removed. Strive to obtain authority based on past performance. This means, Cancer, that no matter how minor a job may appear, it is necessary to do your best; you are building a track record.

Medical science attracts you. Work pertaining to the home, in aiding families, would appeal to you. Many obstetricians, plastics craftsmen, prominent chefs, restaurant owners, poultry raisers, naval officers, and nurses were born under Cancer. Other appealing occupations for you are: farmer, china or glass manufacturer, milk company executive, personnel director, and real estate expert.

The Cancer Hand

Some astrologers are proficient at guessing Sun signs; that is, they can look at an individual and perceive his, or her, zodiacal sign. This is no easy task—it requires experience, practice. The reason is that the Rising Sign (at the time and place of birth) affects personality and appearance, as does the sign the Moon occupied at birth. Yet, the place of the Sun is a strong indicator where character and appearance enter the picture.

Over the years, I have found that one significant key in this effort is the human hand. A person's hand often reveals whether that individual was born under a Fire, Earth, Air, or Water Sign.

You, Cancer, were born under a Water Sign; Cancer belongs to the Water element. The Water Sign group, in a majority of cases, appear to have oval-shaped hands. These include Cancer, Scorpio, and Pisces. In the Water Trinity, the palm is inclined toward fleshiness; the fingers tend to be thick.

Your hand, the Cancer hand, is soft; the mounts under the fingers are highly developed. Your hand bears out your Cancer characteristics; you are impressionable, psychic. You seem able to perceive the thoughts, moods of others.

CANCER SECRETS

The Horoscope, with its twelve angles or Houses, covers every area of life, including your secrets. The Twelfth House holds sway over secret fears, fantasies, undercover problems, all that is hidden or beneath the surface.

In your case, Gemini occupies your Twelfth House; the Mercury of Gemini combines with your Moon Solar ruler to stress emotionalism. The first part of you to be affected by the unforeseen is your stomach. You, more than other persons, must take special care in eating, drinking habits. And the source of upsets is, very likely, relatives. This applies especially to brothers, sisters, and other persons who are closely related to you.

You exhibit a tendency to fear a lack of security. You can visualize what you want, what should be done. But, even after your "vision" becomes a fact, you tend to doubt, to have misgivings.

The closer you are to a person, the more vulnerable you feel; this is natural and it should not provoke fear. But, with you, it apparently does so. You wonder and worry about whether the person in question really understands, perceives, detects what you are and where you are going—you brood and worry about comprehension, *understanding*.

One of your secrets is a fear that you are not communicating. It is your desire—almost an obsession—to make known your views, goals. When others, especially your mother or brother or sister, respond with less than enthusiasm, you fall into a trap of depression.

You tend to "pick up" thoughts. When others cannot match this ability, you fear that you are "on your own." You cannot understand why you can see so clearly while others continue to grope.

A basic secret is that you want to be a go-getter. But you feel that family and other obligations are holding you back. This creates a kind of guilt reaction. You say to yourself, in effect, that you should love and be devoted to your family or other responsibilities. Yet, inwardly, you strive to be on the move, to make snap decisions and to have orders filled, carried out. This represents a conflict. The conflict is between what you *secretly* feel and what you think you *should* be feeling.

What you must avoid in this area is self-deception. It isn't that others are not sympathetic; it is that you don't believe they understand. Once you can eliminate a cloud of self-doubt, you will be able to function more efficiently on an emotional level.

It is not necessary to think that relatives are perfect in order to love them. You can love and continue to experience conflict. Once this factor is recognized, you will be a psychologically healthier person. Break the bonds which tie you to family obligations. You can do this by recognizing a valid obligation and separating it from an imagined one.

Your basic secret is *resentment* toward your role within the family circle. Instead of brooding about it, recognize that you may have a perfect right to feel rebellious in this area.

Leo

July 23 - August 22

Birthstones
Sardonyx and Ruby

Flower
Gladiolus

Numbers
1, 9, and 8

Colors
Orange and Gold

Parts of Body
Back and Heart

Cities
Rome, Bath, Portsmouth,
Prague, Damascus, Bombay,
Chicago, Hollywood,
Philadelphia

Countries
France, the Alps, Italy,
northern Romania

YOUR CHARACTER AND LIFE

Many people have many views about Leo: some are charmed, insisting that Leo is warm, entertaining, dynamic, a natural showman. Others, just as insistent, claim Leo is stubborn, fixed, tyrannical, domineering, a plain ham.

Somewhere in between lies the truth. You are charming; you are a natural showman. And you are also the executive type, preferring to make your own decisions, to arrive at your own conclusions, to be independent. You are forceful, this causes many to comment that you "come on too strong."

Without you, however, there wouldn't be much spice to life, much entertainment, much to debate about, there would be fewer laughs, too. Leo—the natural fifth sign, ruled by the Sun, belongs to the Fire element. It's a fixed sign connoting a bright personality, associated with sex, children, entertainment, as well as royalty. Yes, you will be delighted to know that astrologers refer to Leo as a "royal sign."

You love to be flattered. Flattery will get one everywhere with Leo. Someone could make a ludicrous pronouncement—but you are apt to go along with it—*if* it contains due appreciation of your accomplishments.

Listen: you're no fool. It is just that your ego needs attending. It is just that you are affectionate, you need affection. When it is forthcoming you respond like a thirsty man offered water on a burning desert. Flattery, to you, is a form of affection. Leo is love and Leo is sex. And, being Leo, you are creative, original—often a thorn in the side of orthodoxy. You break conventions, you defy rules;

but instead of being destructive, you usually come up with answers. You build, create, entertain, illuminate, provide light as well as heat.

You're no fool, but you can be deceived—especially by the opposite sex. You have numerous affairs of the heart; some leave emotional scars. How you love the spotlight! You bask in it, revel in it, perform in it, grow in it and, for all practical purposes, even *live* in it. You do, as a matter of fact, *come alive* when performing, holding forth, explaining, expounding, illustrating, demonstrating.

You're in love with love. You give of yourself—but also expect plenty in return. You're not selfish but you can be a selfish lover. Your love of luxury can cause some to regard you as lazy. This is not true, but you can be a lazy lover. You *expect* to be catered to, waited on, *pleased.* You have such an abundance of personal magnetism that the opposite sex spoils you. You love a challenge. You are creative enough to come out "winners."

Many astrologers are guilty of catering to you. That's because Leo entertains and sustains us. But you can be stubborn, at times arrogant. You can be childish rather than romantic, foolish rather than imaginative. All depends, of course, on whether you react to the positive or negative aspects of your sign; much depends on your entire horoscope, based on year, month, day, hour, and place of birth. But, Leo, your Sun Sign is the engine of the chart. Your Leo qualities shine through—and there will be a flash of self-recognition as you study these revelations.

Leo Durocher and Helen Gurley Brown are good Leo examples and so, too, is the inimitable Mae West. Has anyone ever heard the brilliant, colorful Mae West say she would be down to see you? No . . . it's always *you come up and see me sometime!*

Leo can be the bon vivant: witty, urbane. But basically, Leo is associated with the heart of matters. Among other things, Leo is the sign of love, romance, speculation, creativity. Leo is attractive to the opposite sex. Leo is magnetism, fire, shooting-from-the-hip. Born under this dynamic sign, you are impulsive; you have a knack for drawing attention to yourself. You are the showman, the producer, the individual who is able to entertain, explain and popularize even the most abstruse subjects.

On the negative side, you attempt to substitute showmanship for real knowledge. You become superficial, trying to cover up with quips, explanations, frills, bright colors, sayings.

You have numerous affairs of the heart; life is love for Leo. But you tend to experiment, to defeat your own purpose by flitting from one person to the next. This is not, as might be supposed, because your sexual appetite is voracious. Rather, it is a seeking for fulfillment. If you're immature, your ego needs building. Otherwise, fulfillment comes in the form of finding someone who appreciates, shares, laughs, loves, is articulate (especially in praise of you!).

Loneliness is something you despise. In this, you are not unique. But you are especially sensitive in this area, appreciating the spotlight of attention as you do. Your basic nature is romantic. At times it is difficult for you to distinguish between illusion and reality. This is especially true where you—and love—are concerned. You find someone, only to feel the search is beginning instead of ending. You continue to attract colorful persons, bizarre situations. As a result, you're often worn out at a relatively early age because you do burn the candle at both ends.

Am I being too harsh? Well, the purpose of these revelations is to help you to know yourself—the favorable side, and otherwise. The sooner you become familiar with Leo, the better. One does not speak harshly to an individual who has no sensitivity or perceptiveness. You have both—in abundance. You know what is right, even though you often do the wrong thing. You can sense who is good for you, although you often choose someone else.

Leo, you are popular, irresistible, flamboyant, extravagant, colorful, talented. You are bright and shining, inviting; you *demand* experience.

Listen: you are attracted to luxury. You want the good life, the cost is secondary. Extravagance is a key word. Then, one day, you wake up to ask, "Where did the money go?" Fortunately, you possess remarkable recuperative powers. Your stamina enables you to come back, to think on your feet, to utilize showmanship, to make the old appear new and interesting.

On the negative side, the love of luxury can turn to a kind of self-indulgence, or to laziness. You want others to be aware of you and this is expressed in a kind of languid, subtle sort of demand. Carried to extremes the demand becomes a *whine*.

Maturity should be your goal, no matter what your chronological age. Your potential is tremendous if only you make an effort to achieve it. Your imagination is highly developed; you can be a creative person who writes, paints, depicts the character of our time, makes our "place" entertaining, alive, stimulating. You *can!*

Leo is associated with the back and heart, and you do put your heart into projects. Often you are too idealistic almost taking it for granted that others will understand that your motives are pure. And, Leo, just as often, you are apt to have a rude awakening. You discover that animosity has been aroused, that others can be jealous—that they can smile to your face but seethe inwardly with resentment. Then, when the opportunity presents itself, they strike. And you are dumbfounded. You wonder *why*. But, as you mature, as you gain experience; you learn not to lead with your right. You learn, in other words, to keep your guard up.

You have pride. It can be your greatest asset—and fault. You are creative—you want to start from scratch and build. You would tear down tradition if it kept you from expressing yourself. You are loyal; you expect others to display this trait also. Unfortunately, some feel that they have been slighted. Your Sun significator has been too hot to handle . . . and some relationships cool before you are aware of it.

The same applies to your love affairs . . . too hot not to cool off.

The late, great astrologer Grant Lewi said this about you: *Leo . . . is not one to hide his light under a bushel. He wishes to be seen, to be recognized . . . to take his part in the world which he loves, and as return of his love of the world the necessary complement is that the love, respect, esteem of the world come back to him.* Grant Lewi also said that if Leo loves a woman, her love must complement his . . . if he loves the world, the analogy holds.

Grant Lewi concluded by saying that Leo, at his best, merits recognition, and expects to get it, which is a significantly different matter from the negative Leo seeking recognition as an end in itself.

Listen, Leo: *you want to be something, to amount to something, to be known, and to be recognized.* You adore the good things, you want fame, you appreciate it in others, but you tend to construct idols and you tend to be an idol in the eyes of others. By the same token, some would like to see you topple. Often, on the negative plane, you aid the latter—by overindulgence, by becoming complacent, by being fixed in your views, attitudes—by taking it for granted that your light will always shine even if no step is taken to recharge the battery.

When I consider your sign, Leo, I know you have an abundance of so-called natural talent. You are attractive—you want to lead the way. But it is possible that you neglect details or fail to learn your job from the bottom up. You then feign impatience, lack of interest. You say, in effect, that's too easy for me even to attempt, or too boring, or too elementary. It is important that you be truthful with yourself. Leo, when you face the truth squarely, you must try to do something about correcting faults which include lack of patience, an inability to handle mechanical or other subjects which require ability to concentrate.

Actually, there is no real lack of ability. It is a matter of negligence, You skip your homework; you skip the intricacies. You can concentrate, but instead you often swagger.

Leo

You see, Leo, you are great when it comes to viewing projects as a whole. But you can neglect essentials. You want others to catch up to you . . . but other people are aware of details, may not want to skip ahead blithely. It is up to you to help, to exhibit a greater degree of patience, sympathy.

One of your greatest needs is recognition. Listen, Leo: it is no secret that you require praise, appreciation, a pat on the back. Physical contact, in fact, is of extreme importance to you. You are passionate, giving—and, Leo, you expect others to respond. And you want that response in *your way*. You are often too receptive when it comes to affairs of the heart. And also, Leo, I must tell you that you have a tendency to become comfortable. You want others to do the work, to win you, to praise, to warm you up. You want others to bask in your glow when, if the truth be known, you should be doing something to get the fire banked, to get it going, to draw heat from the blaze, not a mere brightness.

You are easily spoiled, maneuvered, put in a position where the fixity of your sign is transformed into a rut. You need change but find change difficult to bring about—you require variety, but you love the comforts of life. Leo, you tend to stay put when your logic dictates that a change is essential.

You love life but make it difficult for yourself to live—and love. One fact can be stated without much fear of contradiction: you don't make it easy for yourself. Everything becomes complicated—humorously so at times, until you become inextricably involved.

Leo

You have a deep, sincere appreciation of the creative arts. You want to be in, you want to be where the action is. You want not only to be part of your time, but to influence the times. Your wants are many—they are complicated, grand, high, expansive, *expensive*. You would be the first to admit that money tends to burn a hole in your pocket. Yet you chide yourself for having so little to show for your efforts. Still and all, Leo, it is difficult for you to learn lessons of thrift, or even temporary self-denial.

You enjoy bright lights, but can feel alone in a crowd. A handshake, a gesture of recognition, of goodwill, from *just one person* can cause you to rise to the heights. You are a natural entertainer, but you want to be something more— you want to be recognized as an interpreter of the times, a writer, a symbol. You can be noble, big in the best sense. You bring entertainment to the world. And you like to laugh. One of your greatest enemies is depression. When you are depressed, Leo, you are like an athlete trying for a hit during a slump. You press, become tense—you seek a confidant. You want not only sympathy, but encouragement, praise. You are never satisfied with halfway measures. When you fight, it's a grand battle. When you love, the sparks must fly, the flames must be ignited into bonfires.

The fires burn bright and hot with Leo. And when the flames begin to flicker, Leo strives to ignite them further. Obviously, you drive yourself. You burn energy. And you must, Leo, *must* learn when to rest, when to get a resuscitation—you must learn how to pace, how to eat, play and work. In short, you must learn *how to live.*

Leo, you could smother the person you love. You almost expect a mirror, the image of *you.* At the same time, you want that person to represent the world. You want to be adored by him or her—in that person you see the world. You, Leo, are obviously not the easiest person to live with, but you do possess assets which many persons consider an equal balance. In other words, you have a way of getting people to put up with you. This is due to your fiery magnetism, due to the fact that you have the unique ability to inspire others, to inspire their confidence in you. These, Leo, are no small assets—they are big ones. In this respect, you are fortunate.

The late, great and inspired astrologer Evangeline Adams said this about you: *people with the Sun in Leo are not only strong themselves, but shed this strength on others. It is,* she said, *the most magnetic of signs . . . perhaps in consequence of this, the disposition is usually masterful and may possibly, in some cases, become almost tyrannical.*

You have so much that you tend to be careless with your assets. Because of this, your generosity can deteriorate into extravagance. Your showmanship can turn into an offensive kind of shrill cry amounting to, "Never mind him . . . listen to me."

You are in danger, Leo, when the challenge is gone, when your job or lover becomes too easy. Sensing this, without being able to put your finger on it, you tend to make things difficult for yourself. You complicate your life, your loves. You become careless, both with your money and your energies. When this happens, you could go to extremes, including overeating, drinking too much, over-responding emotionally. Check your motives, your feelings, your thoughts, ambitions. Locate your actual goal—aim for it, not for something else. There is no need for you to miss the mark. The only person who causes you to go off-track is you, Leo. Don't be sidetracked because you feel your need for self-expression isn't being fulfilled. Be constructive . . . move in the right direction, do something to correct the situation. This is a far cry from merely doing *anything* to shake people up.

Leo, I think you have a positively uncanny talent for creating unhappiness for yourself. You don't seem able to bask in the present, to appreciate it. Instead, you look back to the past, or ponder about the future. But, Leo, what about today—*the "right now" of it?* Let the past lie buried. Permit the future to unravel, to come, to unfold, to make its appearance. After all, you will agree that you can't cause water to boil any faster by staring at it and becoming tense.

You do become tense; you are impulsive. You want to be an original, a leader—not a carbon or a follower. When impulse dominates logic, you lose. Check recent incidents: the odds are that, when your patience flies out the window, you do something stupid. Or you take no action when you *should* be doing something.

You are a natural showman. You love an audience; you are at your best when the pressure is on, when the chips are down: you are a *money player.* You usually are able to back up assertions. You keep something in reserve. You also are a gambler. Speculation, excitement—the wheel of fortune spins and you are there, ready to place a bet on where she stops.

Something is usually happening around you, *involving* you. When the lights dim, when the party is over, you are willing to face the music, but this doesn't stop you from seeking another "party."

You want to be surrounded by glamour, color, by persons out of the ordinary. You can appreciate the artist, the prizefighter, the writer, the actor. You love variety. Your personality is bright enough to attract those seeking to hitch their wagon to a star. A star! That's a magic word with you: star quality, a headliner. What you do must be different, what you own must be unique—what you say must challenge.

A friendship, to you, is not based on what someone can do for you. It usually is a matter of what you can do for the other person. A rare quality—but you possess it. Ironically, this arouses resentment. Those you aid are not above turning on you. Know this and temper generosity with common sense.

Writing, talking about Leo is akin to trying to capture a bright, shining and twinkling star. It is here, there and everywhere: it is elusive and evasive. You can see it. But you can't put your finger on it. That's often the way you perceive yourself. You have a tendency to lose all sense of timing when it comes to placing your affections properly. You meet the right person but at the wrong time. You are generous, giving, a romantic lover, but, very often, with the wrong person. Analyze this quality; find out what it is within you that triggers this kind of situation. One astrological expert claims this may be due to misplaced affection, unwise, impetuous lovemaking.

THE LEO LOVER

Here are some hints for women about Leo men: the Leo man attracts women with unique personalities, talents, problems. A Leo man is fiery, romantic. He demands attention, can become jealous, offended, or aloof if he feels you regard him as anything less than kingly. Remember, it is not enough for the Leo man to be good at what he's doing—he also wants to be told he's good. He is a sucker for flattery. He is warm, affectionate. You can twist him around your little finger if you tell him he's great. The Leo man is attractive to women—he likes to have them around. The best way to hold the Leo man is to be dramatic, *in a quiet way.* He is fascinated by subtle women. If you shout, if you are crude . . . you could lose him. But try this: wipe away a tear, then hold up your chin as if nothing happened. Be sure, however, that he sees you wipe away that tear! He'll melt—he'll change from a lion into a purring kitten. Listen, he's a rather impossible man. He wants to be proud of you. He believes in equal rights for men and women, but he expects you to believe he is just a bit superior and wants you to show it by a subtle squeeze of his hand. I said he was difficult, even impossible, but at least you've now had fair warning!

Here are some tips for men about Leo women: these women have a flair for the dramatic. The Leo woman is not interested in the humdrum, the ordinary, the routine, or the sameness of anything. The Leo woman lives life as if a spotlight were turned fully on her. This is not to say that she is an exhibitionist—but she wants you to be *aware* of her.

The Leo woman is sensitive, alert, dramatic—she wants you to be demonstrative. A touch, a gesture, an expression—a secret signal—these are important to a woman born under this sign. Stand up when she enters a room.

Request her favorite song. Smile in a special way—make it plain that what you do is especially for her. Let her know she occupies your thoughts. The Leo woman's personal magnetism is strong. She attracts the opposite sex. Know this and make yourself a fascinating challenge. All of this may tire you . . . but you learn and live . . . and love . . . through your relationship with a Leo woman.

YOUR RISING SIGN

All persons born under your sign are not exactly the same, although basic characteristics will hold. A horoscope, in actuality, is a map of the sky based on the time and place of birth. If you are aware of your birth time, here are some variations it may cause in your life and character:

Born between 4:00 and 6:00 A.M., your Rising Sign is apt to be the same as your Sun Sign—Leo. This emphasizes your Sun qualities, highlights your romantic nature. You can be generous to the point of being foolish. Control a tendency to be extravagant. With the qualities of your sign magnified, you could be insistent on personal attention. You can demand flattery, which in effect, amounts to expecting subservience. This "double dose" of the Sun causes you to appear selfish. You could, unless you take the trouble to check it, be one who "hogs the spotlight." Others, quite naturally, become resentful. Know this and do something about it. Try staying in the background. It makes for a nice change of pace!

Born between 6:00 and 8:00 A.M., your Ascendant is apt to be Virgo, giving Mercury as your ruling planet. This combines with the Sun significator to make you "sharper" than the average native of your sign. You remain a romantic, but are more discriminating. You remain a showman, but are more industrious. You are more of an analyst; you are aware of the consequences of your actions. Your memory is better than that of many who share your sign. You can learn lines as well as write them. You are meticulous. Life can be a grand design, but you know where the lines connect. You are more apt to be logical than is the average member of this zodiacal group. You can take better care of yourself, especially where diet is concerned.

Born between 8:00 and 10:00 A.M., your Ascendant is likely to be Libra, giving Venus as your significator. This combines with your Sun to make you all but a hopeless romantic. You often deceive yourself in affairs of the heart. You see members of the opposite sex as you wish they might be. This is not the same, always, as being realistic. You are buoyant, but have a distinct tendency to brood. You desire perfection, but encounter flaws. You are aware of aesthetic values; you appreciate art, drama. You could have a remarkable sense of rhythm. Your voice could be unusual. You are aware of your appearance, which is often dramatic. That is to say you stand out in a crowd. You are gentle but insistent. You are especially attractive to the opposite sex.

Born between 10:00 A.M. and 12:00 noon, your Rising Sign is apt to be Scorpio, associated with Pluto. This combines with your Sun ruler to make you more intense than the average native of your sign. Love is a requisite; without it you are lost. Your intuition is highly developed. You sense it when something of importance is about to occur. You time your moves. You analyze, perceive. Your magnetism draws others to you and results, at times, in bizarre situations. You are willing to tear down in order to rebuild. You could do a little better in public relations. At times, people misunderstand your intentions. Thus, you create opposition where none should exist. Take time to evaluate, to explain.

Born between 12:00 noon and 2:00 P.M., your Ascendant is likely to be Sagittarius, giving Jupiter as your ruling planet. This combines with the Sun to provide a talent in you for attracting riches. You are generous, extravagant—but usually you can afford it! It's important to combine imagination with a sense of practicality. You are fond of travel; you are adventurous in dining habits, preferring foreign foods. Much interest is indicated in publishing, advertising, the theater. Unless you are expressing yourself, happiness is elusive. When you do write, speak, set policies, you are at peace within. Know this and be true to yourself, to your potential. You are idealistic, much aware of social justice—or the lack of it.

Born between 2:00 and 4:00 P.M., your Rising Sign is apt to be Capricorn, associated with Saturn. This combines with the Sun to make you more persistent, patient than the average native of your sign. Your influence is far-reaching. Your ally is time. Eventually, your ideas are accepted. You are withdrawn when compared to others in your zodiacal group. You tend to give more of a somber appearance. You can be calculating. You exhibit a sense of responsibility. You are reliable; others confide their problems. The key is to be sympathetic, helpful without becoming inundated. You possess qualities which add up to universal appeal. Don't waste them! Instead, spread your influence, stick to your principles.

Born between 4:00 and 6:00 P.M., your Ascendant is apt to be Aquarius, ruled by Uranus. This combines with the Sun to make you energetic, adventurous, more inventive than is the average native of your sign. You love freedom, especially in the area of expression; thus, you are an innovator, in style, writing, fashion. You would excel as a feature reporter, digging up odd facts, spotlighting people involved in unusual endeavors. You compel attention. You communicate thoughts, ideas; you are a trendsetter. You are altruistic; you become involved with unusual subjects, including astrology. Control your impulses. Think with your mind as well as your heart. You are excellent at analyzing character and are a natural psychologist.

Born between 6:00 and 8:00 P.M., your Ascendant is likely to be Pisces, associated with Neptune. This combines with the Sun to make you sensitive, aware, psychic, capable of being at the right place at the proper time. It attracts you to speculative enterprises; you would make a fine stock-market counselor. You also are a natural actor; you can create moods, atmosphere. You are more pliable, flexible than is the average native of your sign. You have hidden resources and each person sees you in a different light. It's difficult for you to be boring because you constantly startle yourself. You appreciate security, but find it difficult to be practical with your own money. You are excellent at protecting the assets of others, but are willing to take a chance with your own possessions.

Born between 8:00 and 10:00 P.M., your Rising Sign is likely to be Aries, associated with the planet Mars. This combines with the Sun to make you forceful, dynamic. You are courageous, willing to take a chance. You drive hard, work hard, play hard—seldom do you do anything halfway. When your enthusiasm is aroused, you go all out. You're too impulsive, at times, for your own good. You accept challenge—others may think you have a chip on your shoulder. You are aggressive, more so than most in your zodiacal group. Your fiery romantic nature makes you attractive to the opposite sex. It also causes you, at times, to become involved in triangle love situations. You are independent, original: you lead rather than follow and inspire more timid souls to try something different.

Born between 10:00 P.M. and 12:00 midnight, your Rising Sign is likely to be Taurus, associated with Venus. This combines with the Sun to make you a perfectionist. You can be stubborn. You must learn to be more versatile. You are more practical than is the average native of your sign. You are also more capable of saving money. Once you sight a goal, you take action to attain it. You are not as flashy as the classic native, but you are thorough. In romance, however, all your good resolutions can go by the wayside. You are idealistic, artistic, often naive—where the opposite sex is concerned. When it comes to work, you are indefatigable. You organize, plan, build, create a solid base. Learn also to relax. You need a creative hobby.

Leo

Born between 12:00 midnight and 2:00 A.M., your Ascendant is apt to be Gemini, ruled by Mercury. This combines with the Sun in an agreeable manner: you are bright and attractive but often impatient, tending to scatter your forces by having too many irons in the mental fire. Your mind races ahead; you know what others are thinking, what they are going to say. Your attention span is short, often causing you to miss subtle nuances. But you get the gist of affairs, you are in the thick of current events. You are eloquent, have a sense of drama and, when you speak, people listen. Be positive of your facts and you earn respect. If superficial, you are regarded merely as being entertaining. Your personality is ingratiating; you make friends, influence people with ease. You can sell ideas, products—and yourself.

Born between 2:00 and 4:00 A.M., your Rising Sign is likely to be Cancer, ruled by the Moon. This combines with the Sun to make you an intriguing individual. The opposite sex might find you irresistible. This is because you have innate understanding of both men and women—your sense of humor is delightful. You are vivacious, able to project your personality. You are more aware of finance and business than is the classic native of your sign. You love luxury and know how to obtain what is required. You are capable of saving for the proverbial rainy day. You seldom are caught short, either on funds or when it comes to "something to say." You are creative, love good food, and would find being a chef an excellent avocation. Because you express yourself so well, the field of writing should not be ignored.

Leo Friends and Partners

Leo is harmonious in relation to Gemini, Libra, Aries, and Sagittarius. With another Leo, it is a question of who is going to give up the spotlight. Two individuals born under Leo, when together, represent charm, entertainment, and personality plus. But it could be too much of a good thing. To make the relationship succeed, each Leo must be willing to step back, to permit the other to show off special talents, and abilities. Leo is not favorably aspected to Aquarius, Taurus, or Scorpio. Leo is generally neutral to Cancer, Virgo, Capricorn, and Pisces.

Leo Careers

Your Tenth House, that section of your Solar horoscope associated with career, is Taurus—signified by Venus. You are a natural showman—you are attracted to the theater, to entertaining. However, most important, you are a "director." Not only in the sense of a theatrical director (including motion pictures and television), but in the sense that you set policy, decide, are an executive. In plain words, it is best for you to give rather than to receive orders.

The key is proper preparation. You are weak when you skip over essentials. This must be repeated: you should learn the rules before ignoring them. It is when you substitute flash, showmanship, for the rudiments that you get into difficulty.

Listen: you also are a speculator. You enjoy gambling, the excitement of a clash of ideas—pitting your decisions against the game, whether the game be roulette or business. As a matter of fact, you prefer making a game of your activities. (Being in the toy manufacturing business would appeal.)

Naturally, the occupations of actor, entertainer, theatrical director or manager are high on the list for you. The stock market, with its exciting possibilities and element of chance, also appeals. With proper training, you would make an excellent broker or financial counselor.

The vocational factors of your Solar horoscope indicate that you are a natural to achieve success in the theater, in writing and in other fields where creative expression is involved. Other Leo occupations include: entertainment director, heart specialist, child care specialist, or playground director.

Success and Leo go together; so does extravagance. Avoid going too fast, asking for too much, too soon. And keep business separated from emotional conflicts involving the opposite sex!

THE LEO HAND

Some astrologers are proficient at guessing Sun signs; that is, they can look at an individual and perceive his, or her, zodiacal sign. This is no easy task—it requires experience, practice. The reason is that the Rising Sign (at the time and place of birth) affects personality and appearance, as does the sign the Moon occupied at birth. Yet, the place of the Sun is a strong indicator where character and appearance enter the picture.

Over the years, I have found that one significant key in this effort is the human hand. A person's hand often reveals whether that individual was born under a Fire, Earth, Air, or Water Sign.

You, Leo, were born under a Fire Sign. Leo belongs to the Fire element. The Fire element signs are identified by hands that are comparatively small. These hands are cone-shaped, with the palm larger than the fingers, combined. The hand of Leo is broad at the base and tapers toward the fingers.

Incidentally, the Fire Sign group can, at times, also be distinguished by high foreheads. The Fire signs are Aries, Leo, and Sagittarius. There is a tendency for the hair, in men, to recede, giving these natives an intellectual appearance.

A broad base, tapering to a cone with the fingers: that's the Leo hand, not too large. Leo sees projects as a whole and leaves the details to others. This type of person has a small hand in comparison to those who handle details.

LEO SECRETS

The horoscope, with its twelve angles or Houses, covers every area of life, including your secrets. The Twelfth House holds sway over secret fears, fantasies, undercover problems, all that is hidden or beneath the surface.

In your case, Cancer occupies the Twelfth House, ruled by the Moon. This combines with your Sun significator to promote a scattering of forces. One of your great fears is the realization that you don't always know what it is you truly desire—a fear in the sense that you feel a lack of security. Your basic secret, in the deepest sense, is that you want the solid, the home, the established and the conservative, while, at the same time, acting as if you needed the exact opposite. You are the bon vivant who would want a home and faithful mate to come back to—but you still want the freedom to experiment, to display your prowess with the opposite sex.

Another secret is a fear that there will not be enough for that proverbial rainy day. This displays itself in the apparently extravagant way you purchase food to put away "for when we have extra company."

You want plenty on hand. You want to look in the cupboard and find it well-stocked. You fear being forgotten: nothing is more of a blow to your ego than a silent telephone, an empty mailbox.

This helps explain some of your extravagance. It is not that you want to be ostentatious; it is that you want to build a supply, a storehouse, to have plenty on hand . . . for that time when there might not be available cash, or for when the weather is so inclement as to make it impossible to go out and buy, or be entertained. That's one of your best-kept secrets, this fear of being without, of being caught empty-handed.

Another secret is doubt about your own knowledge: you feel you lack some basics. Your education could have been cut short. You may not have done enough reading, study, preparing. Now, for Leo to admit a lack of knowledge represents a monumental effort. That's why this is one of your secrets. A secret desire is to return to school—to get the rudiments, to polish strong points and to eliminate the weak ones.

Basically, however, your secrets are of the constructive variety. That is to say, you do not harbor secret hate or secret prejudice. Your secrets run along lines of self-improvement—generally, for the purpose of making others happier. You do not seek self-aggrandizement, as many might suppose.

While you spend freely, you secretly are concerned with the budget—about what tomorrow might bring. That's why, Leo, you are likely to carry a full load of insurance, medical and otherwise. This represents a contradiction: extravagant Leo on a spending spree secretly aware of costs, effects, credits, and debits. You secretly prefer a good cook to glamour, a basic approach to scattered efforts. While you love a party, you wonder about who is going to clean up the next day!

You secretly admire those born under Cancer and admire the Virgo virtues of cleanliness. Secretly, you want to be admired as a great lover who has a packed library—who reads as well as displays the books. You want to appeal to all segments and to fill lives with joy.

That insecurity concerning enough money and food can be overcome by a basic change of habits—or through the hiring of a good accountant or business manager.

Virgo

August 23 - September 22

Birthstone
Sapphire

Flower
Morning Glory

Numbers
5, 3, and 9

Colors
Gray and Navy Blue

Parts of Body
Intestines and Sympathetic
Nervous System

Cities
Los Angeles, Heidelberg,
Boston, Jerusalem,
Toulouse, Paris, Strasbourg,
Lyons

Countries
Brazil, Turkey, Crete, part
of Greece, West Indies,
Switzerland

Your Character and Life

You are fastidious, diet-conscious—well aware of food value and lack of it. You are the adviser, the editor, reporter, teacher, the harbinger of "new truths" and one who performs basic services, even though many do not appreciate, even rebel at, being told what's best, what's good for them, what's essential to their welfare. Perhaps you, Virgo, are the most misunderstood of the signs. You are analytical, neat, knowing where this and that belongs—*until you rebel.* Then plans go out of the window and that much-heralded "neatness" is transformed into a devil-may-care attitude.

One of the most frequent compliments you receive has to do with age and appearance. "You look so young" is the way it usually goes—this applies no matter what your chronological age. You are the one who gets the family fed, or at least *advises* family members on what and what not to eat. While Cancer can concoct fabulous dishes and make a home of the kitchen, you can get in and out and get the food (very likely wholesome, too) on the table. The dishes get washed and dried and put away—and, still, you do not deprive us of your conversation. Like Gemini, you appreciate wit and humor and are generous with praise. Even if *you* do the cooking, you *admire* the way we eat! Which is to say, you flatter us for enjoying your efforts.

Yes, Virgo does serve—Virgo is the natural sixth zodiacal sign, is mutable, of the Earth element, is associated with service, health, employment, pets. You are the perceptive analyst who, very often, does not follow his own advice. You know what's good for others.

Virgo

Some claim you are pleased with the handling of details. However, this is the result of confusion. What you *are* pleased with is work: not necessarily endless details or minor projects, but with building toward a goal, or achieving an objective. You are restless, mercurial, the opposite of lazy, and you are attractive to the opposite sex. You have a way of making people think that you care specifically about whomever you are talking to, referring to, working for, serving, or aiding. This is an invaluable quality. Used properly you can gain more than some of boasts. You keynote accomplishment.

You have a unique manner of making people identify with what you say, do, even think. You can become indispensable. Those who take you for granted soon learn a harsh lesson: you are not committed to being there, serving constantly. You have your own needs, desires; eventually, you rebel. What you respond to is *kindness*. You will go out of your way to please a thoughtful individual. You will, by reverse procedure, retaliate against one who attempts to exploit you.

Your Mercury ruling planet gives you the ability to analyze, to deduct, and to criticize. When the latter is constructive, you are the theatrical critic, one who knows the difference between art and pretension. On the negative side, you nag. Always, however, with a basic objective: to better the lot, the health, the general welfare of those close to you.

True, many claim you are a critic first and foremost, an individual overly concerned with neatness, vitamins, health, a desire for perfection. I do not agree. Most of your criticism results from a genuine desire to be of service, to improve conditions.

Virgo

Listen: you are not one to be satisfied with the status quo. Your key word is *improvement*. Your desire is progress, not retrogression, You don't take kindly to second-best. You want to be in the forefront and you want a solid base. If the truth be known, you have a keen desire to seek perfection, not only in others, but also in yourself. That, perhaps, is why you place such emphasis on what you eat, diet, health, work. You want the best: your pets are the best—your children, husband, lover, brother, sister—everything and everyone, where you are concerned, can improve, can reach a degree of perfection. In your eyes, the best is attainable, not far away, but within reach, close at hand, and available.

That is you, Virgo, persevering, striving. On the positive side, this yearning, this determination does pay off, for the top can be reached, the best can be achieved if you don't wear yourself, and others, to a frazzle in the meantime.

It must be said, Virgo, that one of your agonizing qualities is this constant striving, without always knowing what it is you want, who it is you desire, where it is you want to be. This accounts for your general restlessness, for what appears to be incessant activity, for your commendable intellectual curiosity, your penchant for "correcting," improving, refining—all the result, in a deep sense, of trying to complete a circle and "come back to yourself." Getting to know yourself is the main objective, whether or not this is obvious. In fact, this revelation could be of immeasurable aid; you can strike a chord of self-recognition. You can perceive why it is you do what you do: it is in an effort to understand you, to know you, to recognize what you are and who you are and where you want to go.

Again, on the positive side, this is favorable, healthy element. On the negative side, however, the doubt turns to uncertainty and leads to a circular movement, around and round, a merry-go-round of activity with nothing solid accomplished.

Your sign, Virgo, is associated with the planet Mercury . . . the fastest-moving planet in the Solar system. Mercury, in turn, is associated with the mental processes. And you certainly are on the move mentally. One of your chief lessons, Virgo, is that of learning to relax. You are two persons. One is the individual we see, the other is the secret you—the one who questions, doubts, chides—the one who can become a victim of what I term *self-nagging*.

Your desire for reason, for order, for cleanliness—when carried to extremes—does lead to self-nagging. You begin by loving and end by criticizing. The closer you are to an individual, the farther you tend to push him, or her, from you . . . by criticizing, improving, adding a touch there and there . . . until, while well-meaning, you have succeeded in erecting a barrier between yourself and the individual in question. This, of course, is the negative side of Virgo, but these qualities are strong in the typical Virgo and, it is hoped, this frankness about your qualities and zodiacal characteristics will lead to greater self-understanding. Armed with *understanding*, you are capable of winning, of achieving, of creating an aura of happiness. So read with care—utilize Virgo traits to be analytical *right now*, listen, perceive, learn, and then apply your knowledge.

With you, the basic tasks get completed and you still have time to read a book. Problems are solved, a dilemma is resolved: and you still have time to hear what others say, claim and plan. You are, in short, indefatigable. You are quick but cautious, not without contradictions, and willing to change your mind if "something better" comes along. You are industrious, discriminating, and precise.

There are numerous celebrities born under your sign, Virgo. Lauren Bacall is one . . . Anne Bancroft is also a Virgo . . . and so are Cliff Robertson and Peter Lawford.

Listen, Virgo: one of your fine traits is the ability to bring order out of chaos, to respond favorably during a crisis—to bounce back, to show spirit and quality, to set an example—even though you may be going through a trying time, or you may need encouragement more than those you are trying to help. You, Virgo, are not easy to defeat because you never give up. You perceive other ways; you get new ideas. You see light where others can only imagine darkness.

One of your needs—a basic part of your makeup—is to be of service. This being so, you tend to attract some persons only too willing to permit you to be of service to them. You must learn to draw the line. Know the difference between being useful . . . and being used.

You test, try, and analyze. You possess an enormous amount of pride. You seldom lower your standards and, because of this, you sometimes find yourself being lonely, or unhappy. You search. What you search for is not always something you can say with certainty. And when you do find it, you don't always know, are not aware, that the search is over.

It's obvious, Virgo, that you don't make life easy for yourself. You are always trying to do something, to be of service. You attract people who use you, who see just how much they can get away with . . . until you get wise, and get hurt. One of your great needs is to be useful. And you are selective. The trouble is . . . you don't always select the right project—or individual. You constantly haunt yourself with the question of, "Am I doing enough?" and, "Is it right?" These are Virgo traits. Unless you control the tendency toward self-doubt, you curb your chance for greater happiness.

You can create a crisis where none exists. You almost seem determined that life is worth living only when there is a problem to overcome, a challenge to be hurdled.

Your existence is ringed with complications, minor and otherwise. You are really in control of what happens, but you don't always realize it. You achieve recognition only to run away from it. You marry only to have second thoughts. You give of yourself only to wonder whether it's worth it.

There is an abundance of inner turmoil, even if it does not show on the surface. You may appear calm, deliberate, calculating, or even cold to some. However, most often, the exact opposite is true, if only outsiders could look inside, beneath the apparent cool exterior.

Your life, your actions can be contradictions. You contradict yourself. You criticize what you really desire. There is a labyrinth of feeling, emotion. You want to be in the thick of things. Yet you pull away. You want to be outgoing, but you are basically shy, perhaps insecure. And that is a key: basic insecurity. To make up for it, to cover it, you put forward a front that appears filled with confidence, security. Inwardly, the opposite is often true.

At times, although you really want to be of service, you can be found shirking duties under the cover of a wise-crack. Obviously, Virgo, you don't make it easy for others to understand or for you to comprehend yourself.

You want to see, feel, touch—you want to *believe.* You are spiritual, but your intellect chides, criticizes, makes you struggle to overcome a natural warmth and innocence. You want to be sure. You think you need assurances, guarantees. You carry a shield which others, understandably, interpret as cool reserve. It is no easy task to rip away the shield, to expose the real you. But it has been done. You could have been hurt and it is likely that you cringe at the memory, chastising yourself, vowing never to let it happen again.

Anatomically speaking, Virgo is associated with the intestines, with the sympathetic nervous system. More than most persons, you are affected by worry, careless diet, excesses. Perhaps the necessity for physical care carries over, making you *emotionally careful,* too.

You want your house in order. You want the best. Your pets are the best . . . so are your children . . . so is your romance. Everything Virgo, tends to fit into a pattern, and when the pieces fly apart, you are there, to put them together again, or to make a valiant effort.

One great asset you can gain from this reading is to learn to praise. If I could tell you one simple thing, Virgo, I would tell you to learn to praise. Turn grumbling into constructive criticism, which also includes praise . . . a pat on the back for a job well done. The more you praise, the less inner turmoil you experience. I am not suggesting intellectual dishonesty. What I am suggesting is that you see through fresh eyes, that you take another look, that you build instead of tearing down.

Here is another clue, one which was emphasized by the late, great astrologer Grant Lewi. *Over-identification of self with work*, he said, *is one of the symptoms that Virgo is going over to the negative side.* Lewi went on to say: *A Virgo woman who is a housekeeper and nothing more, who conceives of herself solely in terms of her duties, is not living on her best side. A Virgo man*, said Grant Lewi, *who talks shop, whose social contacts are altogether or largely confined to business associations, is probably not living on the positive side of the sign.*

And here, Virgo, is another factor which I am sure is important for you to comprehend. It is this: moderation is of extreme importance. And by moderation, I mean moderation even in being true to resolutions. Now, Virgo, this is not as much of a puzzle as it might sound. You see, you have a tendency to go in circles. In resolving to carry out a program, an idea, a promise—you can become overly conscientious. When this occurs, you worry yourself sick trying to carry out a resolution aimed at keeping your health. In other words, you often defeat your own purpose. No one else stops you or stymies you, but you do a pretty good job on yourself.

So, Virgo, when we talk about moderation we mean moderation not only in food and drink—we mean it in the way you do or don't do things. We are talking about your approach to living. You have to let go a bit, to let the ash lie on the rug, to let the job remain half-finished while you complete a thought, a sentence, the carrying out of an impulse . . . including romantic ones.

You have no reason to feel inferior. Yet, Virgo, you become apologetic. You make excuses. You bend over backward to attribute success to luck, to chance or to fate. You don't reveal your emotions too easily or to too many persons. Inwardly, you may be seething, bursting with joy or sorrow . . . but, very likely, you show a calm exterior. This kind of thing, carried to extremes, is one sure road to an ulcer. That's why, Virgo, I say to you: let loose, relax, and don't care too much about whether everything is as neat as a pin.

Instead of being apologetic, or self-sacrificing—move toward the goal of *self-respect.* Bring order, bring a design to your desires. Find an outlet for them and do so without feelings of guilt. Serve yourself, Virgo. That's important, for the keynote of your sign is *service. And the hardest thing* to do is to serve yourself, because, in so doing, you admit respect for self. In order to have self-respect, you have to earn it. And you can't fool yourself because *you* know the truth; you know where you really stand. So, Virgo, the constant serving of others may serve really to cover up your defects, faults, weaknesses. But when you *start serving yourself,* and when you have self-respect . . . you have come along a road which can lead to genuine happiness. Try to perceive the meaning of this—read again, permit the meaning to sink deep into your subconscious.

Pull yourself out of any rut which you may have dug for yourself. See with fresh vision. Appreciate the efforts of others, but also be aware of your own efforts and talents. Stop being afraid of praise, either the kind given others or the kind you may receive from others. You have a way, Virgo, of expressing yourself in a wry, ironic manner. You also have an absolute talent for complicating situations, including your own life. *Perhaps this is because you would rather be troubled than bored.*

You are attracted to difficult tasks and persons. You take a serious view of life, often developing your own philosophy. You constantly prove you are here for more than a laugh, although genuine laughter is, perhaps, your greatest tonic.

Virgo, you are delightful—and a puzzle. You are the critic and the individual who encourages the underdog. You are an enemy of the stuffed shirt and the ally of the poet. You can be practical and imaginative, almost in the same breath, the same second.

Life is a challenge to you because you sense, perceive, and evaluate. You are connected with the times, yet separated. You want to share but you have a shell.

I remember being on a national network television show with a famous Virgo. He stared at me throughout, and didn't direct a word to me until after the show was over. He was Virgo Arthur Godfrey. In typical Virgo fashion, he sized me up. Then he told me that, before his career flourished, a friend whose hobby was astrology predicted—years in advance—the fame that would come, the celebration, the riches, the honors. But Godfrey took his time in telling me this. He wanted, in Virgo tradition, to size me up first, to analyze, to make sure I knew what I was talking about. Then, and only then, would he confide something that was close to him. That's you, Virgo: you collect information, facts—then you spring these things on us when we least expect them—when you appear the least interested or, at best, highly skeptical.

Your friends often ask why you permit this person or that one to use you. And then, almost immediately after uttering this thought, these same persons are making a request, asking a favor. This causes you to wonder, and once more your reserve becomes your shield. You can see through the artificial, smell it out. You can fool yourself, but it really isn't easy for others to deceive you.

You are drawn to mystery. You adore the solving of puzzles. You want and require challenge. In a sense, you exemplify puzzle, mystery, intrigue, a subtle kind of magnetic force.

Greta Garbo is perhaps one of the most famous natives of your sign. She is a good example of one who is health-conscious, diet-conscious—who has an aura of quiet glamour. She is the universal mystery, combined with quiet familiarity and a sense of comedy.

You have an excellent storehouse of knowledge; you can gather facts and figures, only to permit them to lie there, not used. You have all the capabilities, all the instincts for happiness. But you are too willing to let sleeping dogs lie. Wake them up! Make them *serve you*. You will be fulfilling your promise and potential.

THE VIRGO LOVER

I have said of Virgo women that they are discriminating, often regal, very often tiresome in their pursuit of cleanliness and, more often than not, aware of the details of any project one might be considering. Don't underestimate the Virgo woman. She is an invaluable ally . . . she won't let you down if you take her into your confidence. She is mercurial, earthy in nature, energetic, and full of plans. She is ambitious not only for herself, but for the man in her life. Men, here are some special tips, some secret hints for you about the Virgo woman: if you are seeking some kind of half-relationship, she is not the woman for you. But if you are serious, willing to go all the way for her—accept her as a full partner—then she can be a wonderful asset. Confide in her and you will assure her that you are sincere. Keep things from her and she will suspect the entire framework of your character, your motives.

About the Virgo man: I have said that he is demanding. He asks that you prove yourself, that you be willing to sacrifice when necessary. He is not apt to be a sugar daddy. He knows the meaning of work and the value of money.

Now, here are some special secrets, some tips for women about the Virgo man: he wants to feel be is worthy—he is willing to work, to give value for money received. *Integrity* is a key word for this man. He applies his own standards to others, including the woman in his life. He won't tolerate deception. He usually says what be means and be usually means well. This, however, is not always obvious. At times he may appear hypersensitive, overly critical. But he is just being himself and applying his own standards.

YOUR RISING SIGN

All persons born under your sign are not exactly the same, although basic characteristics will hold. A horoscope, in actuality, is a map of the sky based on the time and place of birth. If you are aware of your birth time, here are some variations it may cause in your life and character:

Born between 4:00 and 6:00 A.M., your Rising Sign is apt to be Virgo, doubling the significance of your Mercury significator. This makes you more independent than the average native of your sign. You are dexterous, quick-witted, able to think on your feet. Your ideas are original but you may have too many at once. You seem always to be busy. Your mind races ahead of your actions. You stress personality, appearance, have an abundance of pride. You are not willing to settle for anything but first place and first class. To some, you appear selfish. This is because you know what you want, and, usually, where to obtain it. Your perceptiveness is magnified; so is your restlessness. But, unlike many under your sign, you know enough to fill your own requirements as well as those of others.

Born between 6:00 and 8:00 A.M., your Ascendant is likely to be Libra, giving Venus as your ruling planet. Combined with your Mercury Solar significator, this makes you more intuitive than the average native of your sign. You sense when something of importance is to occur. You get your finger on the pulse of the times; you teach, report, write. You set styles and promote trends. You exhibit vanity because you like beautiful people and consider yourself a person who is special, unique. You exhibit charm—your sense of justice is sharply honed. You are very sensitive to the feelings of others; you help people feel beautiful. Anything, or anyone, coarse revolts you. Unlike many under your sign, your tendency to criticize is softened by a deep need for affection.

Virgo

Born between 8:00 and 10:00 A.M., your Rising Sign is likely to be Scorpio, giving Pluto as your planetary significator. This combines with your Mercury to make you more intense than the average native of your sign. You want to impress and you want to influence; your goals are far-reaching. You are not satisfied to be a big fish in a small pond; with you, it's all the way or nothing. You are courageous, able to sway and influence people. You set examples and others follow. People are drawn to you; you are more sensuous than is the classic native. Others come to you with their problems and you could be attracted to medicine, the healing and psychological arts. You can be secretive and, unless you find an outlet for creative abilities, you "simmer." This means you invite emotional turmoil unless you express yourself—fully.

Born between 10:00 A.M. and 12:00 noon, your Ascendant or Rising Sign is apt to be Sagittarius, associated with Jupiter. This combines with your Mercury Solar ruler to make you more aware of money, material success than is the classic native of your sign. You are also more cheerful. You are extremely fond of travel, but usually return to your place of birth. Your past has a habit of cropping up, reminding you of your obligations; responsibilities play a dominant role. You are not likely to walk away from a family crisis. You can come up with needed funds in time of emergency. Although you return to your place of birth, the travel desire results in numerous journeys and could, finally, find you residing far from your natal place.

Born between 12:00 noon and 2:00 P.M., your Ascendant is likely to be Capricorn, ruled by Saturn. This combines with your Mercury significator to give you great powers of analysis. You are never satisfied merely that something happened; you want to know *why* it occurred. You are perceptive, perhaps more serious-minded than is the average native of your sign. At times, you analyze so long that opportunity escapes. It's important to act on decisions. Your first impressions could be correct. Know this and don't be overcautious. Act on your beliefs; adhere to your principles. You have a way of ingratiating yourself with those in positions of authority. Take advantage of it. Outline goals—present them to important people. You get backing, sometimes more than anticipated.

Born between 2:00 and 4:00 P.M., your Rising Sign is apt to be Aquarius, giving Uranus as your significator. This combines with your Mercury Solar ruler to make you more romantic than is the average native of your sign. You live on illusion; you live for the future and your visions are often prophetic. Desire for perfection, however, could create unhappiness. Learn to appreciate the here-and-now; learn to love what you possess as much as what you might have had or could have in the future. You are "far out" of the crowd, somewhat of a dreamer. Your ideas are considered by many to be eccentric—until you succeed. Then you have more supporters than you desire of the fair-weather variety. You tend to be introspective, but attract friends who are fascinated by your theories of life—and love.

Born between 4:00 and 6:00 P.M., your Ascendant is apt to be Pisces, associated with Neptune. This combines with your Mercury ruler to make you more flexible than the average native of your sign. You tend, however, to scatter your forces. The key is to concentrate, to complete one project at a time. You are also more subtle than is the average zodiacal member of your family. You possess a quiet charm and have a disarming laugh. You also are capable of laughing at your own foibles, which indeed is an invaluable quality. Cultivate it! You are more artistic than the average or classic member of your sign; you are wonderful when it comes to perceiving a project as a whole. But details tend to bore you. You lose interest unless there is challenge.

Born between 6:00 and 8:00 P.M., your Ascendant is likely to be Aries, associated with Mars. This combines with your Mercury Solar significator to make you a natural investigator and pioneer. You are more direct than is the average native of your sign. You have more stamina, can read between the fines and see the fine print. You are perceptive, inventive, capable of making the old appear new. You have your own style, a unique approach, and what you do has the mark of individuality. You're very attractive to the opposite sex; you tend to be headstrong. Once you make up your mind to do something, it usually gets done. At times you rush in where wiser persons fear to tread. You have an excess of energy and would make a fine travel writer.

Born between 8:00 and 10:00 P.M., your Rising Sign is likely to be Taurus, ruled by Venus. This combines with your Mercury Solar significator to make you more intuitive, determined and practical about money than is the average native of your sign. You also are more settled in your views, more receptive and more capable of sticking to a project until it is completed. Your love of luxury could make the budget something of a problem, but you have a knack for coming up with what is needed at the right time. You combine a directness with a kind of soft, subtle approach. You are a natural teacher and can help people develop unique talents. Your practice exceeds that of the classic native of your sign. You are a wonderful ally and a formidable foe.

Born between 10:00 P.M. and 12:00 midnight, your Ascendant is likely to be Gemini, ruled by Mercury, the same significator of your sign. This double dose of mercurial qualities makes you restless, mentally alert, with opinions subject to change at a moment's notice. You are more eloquent than is the average native of your sign. You gesticulate, illustrate points, and many claim you never sit still for more than a moment at a time. Your powers of persuasion are great; you exude a kind of natural charm mingled with humor. Your approach to most problems is original. You can talk your way into and out of almost any situation. You lead an exciting life, similar to being on a merry-go-round; at times, the pace is dizzying. You can write, speak, and act. You do many things well but should learn to concentrate on excellency in one area.

Born between 12:00 midnight and 2:00 A.M., your Rising Sign is apt to be Cancer, associated with the Moon. This combines with your Mercury ruler to make you imaginative and more inclined toward domesticity than is the average native of your sign. You must, however, learn to see people and situations in a more realistic light. You're loyal to your family. You can be taken advantage of by those who play on your sympathy. You're fond of food but aware of diet. You tend to brood, to seek perfection, to wonder about what might be instead of making things happen in the present. Receptive and intuitive, you find new, inviting ways of serving food and making people feel "at home." You often change your mind, but your basic goals remain constant. Your appeal to women is great. You probably are an excellent cook. Men find you comfortable to be with—they often sing your praises.

Born between 2:00 and 4:00 A.M., your Ascendant is likely to be Leo, associated with the Sun. This combines with your Mercury ruler to make you more of a showman than is the average native of your sign. You dramatize. You beautify. You love luxury. You persuade others to buy the best— many accuse you of encouraging extravagance. You could excel in theatrical work, have an unusual speaking voice. You're attractive to the opposite sex and no stranger to romantic involvements. You are artistic, creative; you also attract wealth. You could live on a grand scale, and you ignore petty people and grievances. Instead, you draw to you those who sacrifice for their beliefs. When involved in a project you lift it out of the ordinary and have a knack for gaining publicity and recognition.

Virgo Friends and Partners

Virgo is harmonious in relation to Cancer, Scorpio, Taurus, and Capricorn. Your sign is attracted to Pisces, but many of your qualities and characteristics are in opposition.

You're not harmonious with Sagittarius or Gemini. You're neutral in relation to Leo, Libra, Aquarius, and Aries.

With another Virgo, you see many of your own qualities—some favorable, others leaving something to be desired. The relationship meets a main obstacle in the question of who is to be the dominant force. Two Virgo individuals are apt to clash; each wants to lead, be the critic, and work toward a specific goal. But the goal is not always the same. You have much in common, but on the whole, two under Virgo may find it challenging to harmonize.

VIRGO CAREERS

Your career opportunities are numerous and varied: photographer, teacher, reporter, writer, editor, to name but a few. The Tenth House of a horoscope is associated with occupation, career. This sector of your Solar chart is Gemini, associated with Mercury, just as your Sun Sign is related to that speedy planet. Mercury is mental, the mind; thus, your perceptiveness, intellectual curiosity should play an important role where career is concerned. You personally are annoyed by waste, misdirected talent. You are not so much concerned with reputations or press releases—you want the facts and you judge from actual performance. You would make a fine personnel director because you want others to do their best, and you are ready to reward talent.

In selecting an occupation, bear in mind that you have natural ability to succeed in professions devoted to helping people. This includes medicine, law, social service; you might excel as a teacher, accountant, merchandise manager, buyer, graphologist, editor, printing executive. That's not all for Virgo; the choice is wide. The key is information, communication, a need to be in the thick of significant events. You could succeed in the broadcast industry; your ability to collect pertinent data makes you invaluable in a news bureau.

You need to develop your ideas. You seem content, at times, to track something down—after that, the interest lags. If you learn to follow through the world could become your oyster. You serve, prepare, outline work methods; you are there when the chips are down.

You also might find that the following occupations open doors of opportunity: dietitian, cruise director, draftsman, food checker, hygienist, medical technician.

Listen: it could be that you are the inspiration, the power behind the scenes. You are a troubleshooter; you can support one who is working under a handicap. You are invaluable to an individual who is being tested and requires reassurance. You provide the morale boost and are actually responsible, in many instances, for the success of important projects.

THE VIRGO HAND

Some astrologers are proficient at guessing Sun signs; that is, they can look at an individual and perceive his, or her, zodiacal sign. This is no easy task—it requires experience, practice. The reason is that the Rising Sign (at the time and place of birth) affects personality and appearance, as does the sign the Moon occupied at birth. Yet, the place of the Sun is a strong indicator where character and appearance enter the picture.

Over the years, I have found that one significant key in this effort is the human hand. A person's hand often reveals whether that individual was born under a Fire, Earth, Air, or Water Sign.

You, Virgo, were born under an Earth Sign; Virgo belongs to the Earth element. The Earth element hand is more basic than is the average palm. That is, an Air-type hand would be long, slender, while the Earth hand is more apt to be square rather than elongated. Your hands, Virgo, tend to be wide, rather than long. If other elements of your chart emphasize Earth, your thumb would be stiff rather than flexible. Many under Virgo, however, have thumbs more pliable than the other Earth signs, which are Taurus and Capricorn. Earth Trinity persons are sincere and solid; the "square jaw" is another mark of identity. You are apt to have more lines on your palm than does the average individual; a multi-lined palm is a giveaway for mercurial-type persons, Virgo and Gemini.

If your tastes are earthy, basic, your hand is apt to be of the typical Earth triplicity: square, with the thumb short rather than long.

VIRGO SECRETS

One of your outstanding secrets is a desire to be "sexy," attractive, captivating, ravishing. The horoscope, with its twelve angles or Houses, covers every area of life, including your secrets. The Twelfth House holds sway over secret fears, fantasies, undercover problems, all that is hidden or beneath the surface. In your case, Leo occupies your Twelfth House; the Mercury of your sign combines with the Leo

Sun significator to reveal a need for the kind of security that comes from being admired, needed, *wanted*.

You are likely, also, to carry a secret connected with children, your own or others. You want the best and your pride is a secret, too. When all does not work out according to Hoyle, you build on imagination. You are quite creative at "keeping secrets."

Now, what do we mean by "secrets"? The Twelfth Sector relates to confinement, hospitals, asylums: an area where freedom is restricted. By secrets, we mean a part of you that is confined, that you want to protect from public view. In your case, Virgo, your secrets are apt to be as big as life: having to do with sex, children. Your secrets have to do with clandestine affairs, arrangements, meetings; the romantic rendezvous is part of your makeup, plays an essential role in your life. It is a *secret* part of you, in that most persons would not fathom this area.

Your secret desire is glamour; you fantasize about being in the spotlight, being one who sparkles and whose light attracts the opposite sex. Your inward desires have to do, also, with creativity: you want to stamp your style, to create literature, paintings, which set the pace and initiate the style. Your secrets and fantasies are exciting, to say the least.

Honor, high office, recognition—these desires are also part of your Walter Mitty existence. Your secrets have to do with celebrities; you want to be a confidant, to be intimate enough with the famous so that you are a part of that life, in part of the excitement, the whirlwind activity. Many who know you, Virgo, might dispute this, but *you* are secretly aware of it.

Virgo

Although you are basically intellectual, part of your secret desire is to be completely emotional, to let yourself go, to respond, to be colorful and to possess a devil-may-care attitude. Listen: your secrets are almost the opposite of what you present for us to view. One might suspect that you lead a double life!

Your basic secret is a thirst for glory. Your secret is that you feel you are better than your position indicates, no matter how high you may presently stand on the ladder. This is a "good secret," if you do not become bitter. On the constructive side, you strive to transform secret desires into realities. *And you are capable of obtaining what you imagine.*

You secretly want to be a party girl or a man about town. You want to be where the action is and you are in love with courtship, showmanship: again, the opposite of what outsiders might think you are thinking. You are, in your fantasies, a gambler who wins enormous amounts . . . and spends to give pleasure to loved ones. Secretly, you want to be surrounded by friends: eccentric, talented, romantic, and famous friends.

Listen: you could, as the saying goes, write a book. You should—at least one! That "secret" creative force is bubbling within; let it out in a constructive, creative manner.

You secretly believe in luck and you "know" that your ship is going to come in, that the music will be your tune and that the people will be looking up to you.

Yes, it would be a whale of a book!

Libra

September 23 - October 22

Birthstone
Opal

Flower
Cosmos

Numbers
6, 4, and 9

Color
Indigo Blue

Parts of Body
Kidneys and Lumbar Region

Cities
Antwerp, Charleston, Vienna, Lisbon, Frankfort, Johannesburg, Leeds, Copenhagen

Countries
Austria, Burma, northern China, parts of India, Tibet, Upper Egypt, Argentina, Japan

YOUR CHARACTER AND LIFE

Balance and harmony—those words are descriptive of your sign. This does not at all mean that your life is all harmony and balance. Rather, your thrust is toward the goal of peace and love. In seeking this goal, you often bend backward to avoid conflict. When you do this, you seem to invite difficulty. Others are too willing to step in and give you a little push—over backward, all the way on your back.

You are often accused of procrastinating. In actuality, you are waiting—for the right time and place. Those who appreciate you are fascinated by your sense of beauty and balance, your ability to see two sides of a question.

You were born under the natural seventh zodiacal sign, associated with Venus. Libra signifies cooperation, marriage, partnership, public relations, and it represents a sense of equilibrium. It means that you try to balance good and evil, harshness and beauty; your tastes are delicate and anything coarse repels you. This applies to all areas: love, sex, finance. You would rather hurt yourself than deliberately cause injury to another.

One would think, with your wonderful intentions, that everyone would be "on your side." But that is not the way of the world. You are, it is true, adored by many. But many others find that you are not their cup of tea. All right, you might be saying, that applies to many persons. But, in your case, it is of special significance.

Your planetary significator, Venus, is a symbol of luxury and love, fulfillment and frustration, beauty and the beast. This is a way, Libra, of stating that your life tends to run in cycles: high and low, good and otherwise, happy and sad, prosperous and wanting. The scales of Libra tip back and forth and the maintaining of balance is of the utmost importance, *no matter how the scales sway.*

Your cycle changes, almost without notice—that is, without advance notice. Libra is the Seventh House and this means that there is nothing halfway about you, despite your *desire* to be balanced, to stand in the middle. But, listen: you view the world and the world sees you. Both you and the world can be in love. However, as in the case of lovers, there are "quarrels." You appear to be on a precipice—the height can be dizzying or gratifying. Unless there is a kind of inner balance, you fall—to the delight of some, to the sorrow of others.

Your emotional mechanism is delicate and it is no easy task to put the finger of analysis on you. You see, you move, swing and sway, like a scale; you're capable of moving to and fro with the gentlest breeze. Let's put it this way: you are easy to love, which by the *I Ching* principle means also that you are easy to dislike. You are a captivating individual who craves balance and justice, but who could become involved in something less than beautiful.

Your almost subconscious, innate goal is toward culture. You are a humanist. That being so, you also are very human and subject to human frailties. You can be soft, giving, but also can build resentment and lash out at those who love you the most. You can do things to hurt yourself. You are desirable and sensitive. You can hurt and be hurt. What I'm attempting to establish is that you are *vulnerable.* You are difficult to pin down but you are a natural mediator. You are more skilled in solving the problems of others than in aiding yourself.

Let me repeat, Libra, that your desire is for beauty—your aim is for justice—your need is for love. If I talk about some of your negative aspects, it is because, at times, you become discouraged and revert to self-pity, to a kind of shrugging which says, in effect, "What can I do about it . . . what can I do about anything?" When this happens, you are not living up to the best in yourself.

Many times people lash out at you in a sense of frustration. These responses on the part of others are caused because you challenge them with your display of idealism, and some people feel small in your presence. To justify themselves, they criticize, they try to belittle you, when, if the truth be known, they revere you, and secretly wish to emulate you. This may not be easy to comprehend—all at once. But, Libra, if you will take time to think, to analyze, you will discover the truth of this statement. Read again . . . especially this part. It will, I am sure, help you to understand why those closest to you, at times, seem to want to push you away. What they really want is breathing space, time to digest your example, your thoughts, your principles.

Your Solar horoscope depicts unusual conditions where love affairs are concerned. Your emotions often betray you. Emotions mingle with logic; often they battle each other. You want a home; you desire conditions described as *settled*. Yet, at the same time, there is a hunger for experience, excitement. You contradict yourself and then wonder why those close to you often wear a puzzled expression. You are delightful but exasperating. You attract unusual or far-out people. And, in turn, you are attracted to these persons. You see, Libra, routine people tend to bore you. Routine activity can leave you cold, listless. You revere intelligence. You were born under an Air Sign, in the Air Trinity, which signifies intelligence. I have discovered about you, Libra, that you would rather endure emotional wounds than be bored by one who is so plain, predictable, and practical that he, or she, puts you to sleep.

One of our great authorities on astrology and sex, Vivian Robson, said this about your sign: *The women are romantic . . . and tend to be in love with love rather than with any particular person other than themselves. In common with Libra men, they crave admiration and flattery, even when they know it is merely flattery, for there is no one quite so capable of willfully avoiding unpleasant facts or willfully believing that what he or she knows is untrue as a Libra.* This makes one danger obvious. You tend to judge the worth of people by what they say about you . . . by how much they *claim* they admire you. This, of course, can be dangerous because a shrewd individual could make you dance to any tune.

There are numerous celebrities born under Libra. Among them are Mickey Mantle, Deborah Kerr, Helen Hayes and Brigitte Bardot.

Listen, Libra: you tend to shy away from the obvious. You can be competent, but impractical. Let's put it another way. You are sensible, efficient when it comes to the difficult, the subtle, the challenging question or problem. But, at times, you simply cannot see the forest for the trees. If something—a situation, problem, or person—is obvious, simple, easy to solve, then you move away, in another and needlessly difficult direction. You are capable of interpreting symbols, of detecting trends, of perceiving undertones. But once the trappings are removed, and an earthy situation is involved, you seek other reasons. You become almost synonymous with the proverbial absent-minded professor. Being under the Air Trinity, you prefer the nonobvious. And, because you prefer it, you seek it, are attracted to it, draw it to you. So, Libra, when confronted with a simple, everyday question or problem, you make more of it than is required or deserved. And that is what we mean when we say you can be impractical.

You are a perceptive individual. But you are wide open when it comes to a swinging member of the opposite sex. That is to say . . . one who goes after you, who decides to attract you, to compel your attention. Then, Libra, you are wise but foolish. You are capable but helpless. You are charming but susceptible to charm. You are, Libra—in the parlance of fighting—a sucker for a right.

Libra, you are naive. You are sympathetic, considerate, capable of sacrificing your own desires for the greater good. You are, as we say, all of these things, but you also are *naive.* You think that because *you* adhere to certain principles others, too, adhere to them. Listen, Libra: in plain words: you have an agonizing tendency to leave yourself open to punishment.

Sound is important to you: musical tones, the voice, or the sound of music. These things are meaningful where you are concerned. You can appreciate mathematics, music, the music of the spheres, which means, in this case, the rhythm of the universe, the movements of the planets, the categories of life. You appreciate order, the involvement of one human in the life of another, the meshing of the gears, the give and take of human relationships.

If I were to criticize you, Libra, I would say or ask, "Where is your sense of direction?" You are many-sided, but you encounter difficulty in forming a policy, fixing a viewpoint, or charting a direction. On the negative side you are like a rudderless ship. There is life, action, and movement. The motor is running—but where are you going?

You are attracted to law, order, the arts, various cultures. You involve yourself in justice, civil liberties, the rights of the underdog. But your methods, your touch are often too subtle to be felt. While you want to make an impact . . . you are afraid of making dent. Your love of harmony, of beauty is so great that you pull your punches so as not to intrude on the scene, the picture, the situation, the person. This creates one of two conditions: either you become discouraged, or enamored with the idea that it merely takes time. Anything takes time, if only balance is maintained, if only anger is suppressed. In effect, Libra, you are discouraged, or hopelessly optimistic, which brings us again to the symbol of your sign, Libra: the Scales, balance (the scales of justice, the scales of decision). And so I would say to you: learn the importance of making a decision. I don't care, Libra, which way you decide. But I do want you to make the decision . . . I want you to decide . . . one way or the other.

Listen: once you rid yourself of indecision, you become less subtle and thus more direct. This is the right course, because it relieves anxiety. That's one thing you have in spades—anxiety. Get rid of it by conditioning yourself to decide, to make a decision. Instead of balancing the scales, of incessantly weighing facts—instead of that—decide. When you do begin making decisions, anxiety will evaporate. You will, in turn, begin to relax, to live, to unravel, to be true to yourself, and to be a beautiful human being.

Let's talk, for a moment, about this anxiety of yours—these anxieties. You are anxious about whether you are doing enough. You are anxious about whether you are doing the right thing, *or anything.* The reason is that, perhaps early in life, you expressed your love nature and were castigated, rebuffed, disappointed, disillusioned. And you've been casting about for a reason ever since. You've been rationalizing, making excuses, taking gallops in logic.

You, above all other zodiacal signs, possess much to admire: physical beauty, principles, idealism. And this could make you fair game for the less talented, the coarse, the ambitious, the schemers. But once you become *decisive,* once you obtain a definite point of view, an outlook, then the odds swing in your favor and the result is greater strength, more happiness.

However, you often mistake friendship for love—then you feel guilty because you are not deliriously happy. It is possible for you to love and hate, almost simultaneously. Once you accept this fact and stop feeling guilty about it, you will have advanced in a psychological sense. You will have matured. Remove your emotional armor. Face yourself as you actually exist. Then you'll become lighter, freer, free and easy. For you, this is essential to happiness. And, Libra, if you persist in regarding happiness as something symbolic instead of earthy, you are persisting in making your life one of discord. Seek harmony. Insist on it. Make your life a song which sings instead of squeaks. Harmonize, and get into the rhythm of your own being.

Let's be frank, Libra. You can't play the game both ways. It's either one way or the other—either life or an imitation of life. You are, in actuality, a warm, passionate being. Until you accept this, you are denying a very real, major part of yourself. There is no reason for this self-denial. Start enjoying yourself. Make sure your life is a song that sings.

It is true that you don't necessarily ask for the impossible. Yet you constantly strive for goals that appear out of reach. You become upset by minor details, but you are perfectly willing to view an entire project. You have solutions for major problems, but the minor ones tend to trip you.

You want love in its fullest sense, but you turn your nose up at what you consider the ultraphysical. You listen to the problems of *others* and watch them walk away when you try to express your own. Your Solar ruling planet is Venus and that is associated with love, but also with self-indulgence. Venus is beauty but also involves the very real physical contact between persons in love.

You could excel in law, public relations. You have a way of sensing the pulse beat of the public. You can anticipate needs, moods, desires. You appreciate beauty and can help others to do the same. Often, however, you become involved in matters which are costly, impractical. You have faith in individuals who do not always have faith in themselves.

You are often considered a soft touch. This is so because you permit it to be so. On the other hand, you can be efficient. You can achieve great heights no matter who, or what, stands in your way. The choice, of course, is your own.

You are a willing worker but, at times, you appear afraid to get your hands dirty. I mean this, of course, in a symbolic sense. And I say to you that you've got to learn to get your hands dirty . . . to get involved . . . to give of yourself, to expose yourself, to leave yourself open. Once you do, Libra, you will find that dirt is clean. It is natural—it is our mother the Earth. It is life and, for you, it is necessary to live—so begin right now!

You are an idealist who can move people, *once you commit yourself.* And, once committed, you can attract followers, sway public opinion, battle ferociously for a cause. Your burning need for seeing that justice is done takes you to the forefront of controversial causes. And listen: often you *create controversy* in order to exercise that sense of justice. You rock the scales, and swing them against the wind to demonstrate that balance can be maintained in the face of adversity. You are not satisfied with mere serenity: you feel it must be earned, can only be appreciated in the calm that follows a storm. That's why, Libra, you are not fearful of the odds or of opposition: you run through the line and reach a goal *because* of roadblocks. You appear quiet but you want to earn your way to tranquility.

You can be on top of the world, Libra, but it seems that in order to achieve that height, you must first touch bottom. That's the crux of the matter. That's what, in these words and paragraphs and pages, we have been seeking to say. That is what the Scales mean to you—up and down—or down before you go up—that's the story of your life.

THE LIBRA LOVER

Here are some special tips for men about the Libra woman: love is all-important to her, so are her surroundings. Now, men: carelessness in taste is one way to lose the Libra woman. Listen: she, like all of us, does have her faults. And one of those faults is to be affected in an extreme manner by manners, by outward appearances. Often she is apt to bypass something, or someone worthwhile, because she insists on manners before morals. Perhaps she is taking a leaf out of Oscar Wilde's book . . . and she is very apt to be an admirer of Wilde. Her key words are romance, partnership, marriage, beauty, the independence required to flourish and flower, to develop and to assimilate the beautiful things in life.

The Libra woman's moods can soar all the way to the sky—or sink down to the cellar. She exhibits a tendency to say "show me" while neglecting to prove her own abilities or to explain her motives. Listen, men: the Libra woman expects you to realize her worth, to take for granted that her motives are beyond reproach. In short, she expects you to appreciate without asking, to accept without doubting, to love without bargaining.

Now, to be fair—let's turn to special hints for women about the Libra man. One of the first things to remember, when dealing with the Libra man, is to avoid any display of irritability. The roof may be leaking . . . the bank account could be overdrawn, but he expects you to reassure him, to smile, to be compatible, to exhibit a sense of humor, awareness, and faith. The Libra man seeks a woman who has an even temper, who can laugh in the face of adversity. He is appreciative of talent, art, literature, music. He will encourage hobbies, even if such encouragement costs him money. At times it appears he is not very demanding in the ordinary sense. But there is one thing the Libra man does demand. He demands refinement. Anything coarse makes him shudder inwardly. He may not come out and say it, but when you use language that is of the street variety, when you carp, when you are quick to anger, he cringes. The

Libra man needs to be told how good he is. In this way, he is similar to the Leo man. And when dealing with a Leo or a Libra man, remember this: flattery will get you everywhere. The Libra man has more of a sense of humor than you might at first perceive. He is nobody's fool, although at times he may act like one.

YOUR RISING SIGN

All persons born under your sign are not exactly the same, although basic characteristics will hold. A horoscope, in actuality, is a map of the sky based on the time and place of birth. If you are aware of your birth time, here are some variations it may cause in your life and character:

Born between 4:00 and 6:00 A.M., your Rising Sign is apt to be Libra, doubling the significance of your Venus ruler. More than the average native of your sign, you are capable of seeing the funny side of life. For you, humor is beauty, as are learning, intelligence. You are sensitive, capable of seeing through sham. You are the opposite of pretentious. You can travel far and wide, only to return to the crisis point, to face the music, to settle the issue. You are not a coward, although your gentle demeanor could deceive some into thinking otherwise. You can solve legal dilemmas, even though you might lack formal training. You have an instinct for working out complicated problems—of others. You succeed in joint efforts and partnerships. The twin capacities of a sense of beauty and humor make you one who is envied, admired, revered, resented.

Born between 6:00 and 8:00 A.M., your Ascendant is likely
to be Scorpio, associated with Pluto. This combines with
your Venus significator to make you more self-assertive than
the average native of this sign. You are independent, magnetic, extremely attractive to the opposite sex. You can be
intense; once you decide to do something, there isn't much
that others can do to dissuade you. You can be jealous; you
can seek that which is not your own. You can want money,
but feel you have it coming to you. You are daring, a natural pioneer. And you are willing to take a chance on your
abilities. Some claim you are egotistical. In a sense, you are:
it is a necessary adjunct to your drive, power, and inner
confidence. You know what you want and you strive to
attain it. That's fine, despite what others might claim.

Born between 8:00 and 10:00 A.M., your Rising Sign is apt
to be Sagittarius, giving Jupiter as your significator. This
combines with your Venus Solar ruler to accent idealism.
You are also more apt to be actively engaged in legal matters, more so than other members of your sign. People confide in you. You are called on during times of emergency.
Some take advantage of your tendency to step in where
more timid persons fear to tread. You want to influence
people. That's why self-expression is a necessity. You are
frank, a natural crusader, fond of travel. You could be
active in societies aimed at preventing cruelty to animals.
Your love of beauty is magnified. You revere nature and
are made sick by those who mar natural beauty.

Born between 10:00 A.M. and 12:00 noon, your Rising
Sign is probably Capricorn, associated with Saturn. This
blends with your Venus Solar chart ruler to cause you to

be more cautious and analytical than the average native of your sign. You are able to judge people, situations; this makes you an invaluable asset in closing a business deal. You are shrewd, but tend to brood. You want excitement, but also desire security. You want change, but are hesitant to throw off methods which have been proven by past performances. You have appeal for the opposite sex, but are discriminating. You want the best and often deny yourself. This makes you appear elusive and even more attractive. You are determined and possess the crusader's zeal.

Born between 12:00 noon and 2:00 P.M., your Ascendant is likely to be Aquarius, associated with Uranus. This blends with your Venus Solar ruler to make you inventive, creative, and to give you more drive than the average native of your sign. You can handle responsibility because you usually are creative enough to find alternatives. This means you function best under pressure, much more so than your zodiacal brothers and sisters. You are concerned with rhythm, power; you want things in place, although you give the impression of not caring one way or the other. This is deceptive; it throws others off guard. You know where everything should be, and how it should sound. You could perform complicated tasks, such as conducting an orchestra, without appearing to be under pressure.

Born between 2:00 and 4:00 P.M., your Rising Sign is apt to be Pisces, giving Neptune as your ruling planet. This combines with your Venus Solar significator to make you more perceptive, intuitive than is the average native of your sign. Many claim you are psychic. This may be debatable. But you are *observant.* You notice things that others tend to overlook. You appreciate design. This includes the design in a flower, a snowflake as well as in an architectural structure. You appear gentle, but you are strong when necessary. You can keep a secret and you are romantic. It is not unlikely that you'll become involved in clandestine affairs. You are much more than many would suppose; you know what you are doing even when your direction appears haphazard.

Born between 4:00 and 6:00 P.M., your Ascendant or Rising Sign is apt to be Aries, making Mars your significator. This combines with your Venus Solar ruler to make you more passionate than is the average native of your sign. You have zeal; you are courageous and tend to be headstrong. Often your actions are based on impulses; this applies especially to affairs of the heart. You are dynamic, you possess an abundance of personal magnetism. You are more direct, forthright than is usual for members of your zodiacal group. You are a leader, but you direct with tact. You have a soft touch, but leave an imprint. You are diplomatic, but can apply pressure when necessary. You are enthusiastic; you generate excitement. You would make a fine entertainer because people are drawn to you.

Born between 6:00 and 8:00 P.M., your Ascendant is apt to be Taurus, making Venus the ruler of both your Rising and Sun signs. This emphasis gives you a more sensuous nature than the average native of your sign. You are artistic, but tend to scatter your forces. You are more versatile than might be imagined. Some think you are stubborn, but you can make changes at opportune moments. You know the value of money, but are willing to spend on art objects and luxuries. You treasure possessions. The key is to be sure you are not possessed by them. You collect. You accumulate objects; this makes it difficult for you to move, to change residence. You don't know what to keep, what to discard. You are fond of the social graces, and are an excellent host or hostess.

Born between 8:00 and 10:00 P.M., your Rising Sign is apt to be Gemini, associated with Mercury. This combines with your Venus Solar ruler to make you more of a natural teacher than the average native of your sign. You are active, a nonconformist; you seek adventure and can relate experiences in a compelling manner. That's why you are a gifted teacher and could be a writer. You are a combination of the analyst and the emotional being. People want to hear what you have to say: this makes you an orator; you always have an audience. You are great at ad-libbing. Your sense of comedy is sharply honed. Your thoughts race ahead of your actions. Your intuition is highly developed. You seem to sense what is going to be said; you perceive happenings before they occur.

Born between 10:00 P.M. and 12:00 midnight, your Ascendant is probably Cancer, associated with the Moon. This combines with your Venus significator to make you more intense than is the average native of your sign. You have a knack for handling and earning money; many seek your counsel in financial affairs. You are sensitive, and tend to be moody. You are serious, at times seem so bent on security that you forego relaxation. It's not wise to be tense; learn to loosen the emotional reins. You are loyal, protective, but often you stick with the wrong cause, the wrong people. This means some take advantage of you; they know you come through, and they lean on you. You adore your home and your favorite room is the kitchen.

Born between 12:00 midnight and 2:00 A.M., your Rising Sign is apt to be Leo, giving the Sun as ruling planet. This combines with your Venus Solar chart significator to give you more dramatic ability than the average Libran native. Your feelings run deep and you are capable of expressing them. Much of your world is illusion; thus, you are the artist, writer, actor. You can make us perceive behind the scenes, you assert yourself in positive terms. Often you are lonely, although you are very attractive to the opposite sex. You can be extravagant. You fall in love easily. You are sensitive to the feelings of others. You are a showman. You are many things but you wish you were appreciated to a greater degree.

Born between 2:00 and 4:00 A.M., your Ascendant is likely to be Virgo, giving Mercury as your significator. This combines with your Venus Solar ruler to make you more capable of writing and speaking than is the average native of your sign. You have dexterity; you gesticulate. You are affectionate, possess intellectual curiosity. You are never satisfied with surface indications. You dig deep, you analyze; you want to know reasons. You get to the heart of matters. You are conscientious; you perform services and you are especially fond of sharing knowledge. You apply yourself and you usually are capable of rising above petty details. At times, some consider you a time waster. This is because you don't utilize your time in the accepted manner. You study, contemplate, try new ideas; you are an experimenter and an innovator.

LIBRA FRIENDS AND PARTNERS

Libra is harmonious in relation to Leo, Sagittarius, Gemini, and Aquarius. You are attracted to Aries, but much in the manner that opposites attract each other. Libra is not favorably aspected to Cancer or Capricorn and is neutral in relation to Virgo, Scorpio, Pisces, and Taurus.

With another Libra, you share numerous experiences, many of them beautiful. There's lots of laughter, much art and light, but not too much staying power. This relationship is good for fun and games, but where settling down is concerned, there are apt to be problems. You come down from the clouds to face everyday realities and the relationship undergoes a marked change. It can work, but it requires wisdom, maturity.

LIBRA CAREERS

You desire to give comfort, pleasure, especially to those who appreciate your efforts. Whatever you do, you attract a special clientele. The Tenth House is associated with career; that section of your chart is Cancer. Although artistic, you deal in practical matters. You can make staples appear spectacular. Your sense of beauty and design aid along this line. What you aspire to, you usually achieve. This is because, despite your imagination, you also have a practical touch.

You have a genuine desire to help people. This tendency attracts you to work in institutions, social service. You could succeed as a diplomat, trial lawyer, musician, artist, actor, florist, milliner, society editor, entertainer, perfume manufacturer. Subjects in the fine arts category attract you; you would enjoy being an art museum curator.

Listen: more than for most, music is a medicine for you, a tonic which heals emotional wounds. You are affected by your location and should live and work in a quiet place where activity is creative rather than merely "busy."

The Moon significator of your career sector indicates public recognition for your efforts. Women, especially, are customers and consumers and an audience for what you create. Combined with your Venus, this indicates real profit through doing what you like, creating with a unique, original touch. You successfully manufacture and distribute what you do produce. Fashions which many can afford serve as but one example. You can be a confectioner, cosmetician, furrier, florist, haberdasher, interior decorator, milliner; there is "music" to what you do and music in your place of business is an essential.

Finding the right partner, in marriage or otherwise, is important to your welfare. You have the ability to sense public desires, to *create* those desires. You are an artist, whatever you do. And with someone by your side to appreciate you, you are a world-beater!

THE LIBRA HAND

Some astrologers are proficient at guessing Sun signs; that is, they can look at an individual and perceive his, or her, zodiacal sign. This is no easy task—it requires experience, practice. The reason is that the Rising Sign (at the time and place of birth) affects personality and appearance, as does the sign the Moon occupied at birth. Yet, the place of the Sun is a strong indicator where character and appearance enter the picture.

Over the years, I have found that one significant key in this effort is the human hand. A person's hand often reveals whether that individual was born under a Fire, Earth, Air, or Water Sign.

You, Libra, were born under an Air sign; Libra belongs to the Air element. The Air hand is artistic. It is a triangular hand, best symbolized by the signs Gemini, Libra, and Aquarius. Your hand is marked by narrow palms and long fingers. Your hand is graceful, as contrasted to the Earth type (Taurus, Virgo, Capricorn), which is square and "practical." You are likely to have more lines on your palm than the average hand. You are sensitive, and this produces a lined hand. Basic types, those who work with their hands, have fewer lines. Your hand, the Air hand, denotes one who is intellectual, poised, artistic, sensitive to the moods of others.

Your hands are expressive. You don't use them to gesticulate to the extent that Gemini does, but you do express yourself with your hands. The Libra hand is much longer than it is wide. And it is likely to be a delicate hand, seemingly made for caressing.

LIBRA SECRETS

One of your secrets is a fear that your health is not the best; you fear that there is some connection here involving your appearance, that you might not be particularly robust. If a male, one of your fears (as revealed by your Twelfth House Virgo in combination with your Libra Sun sign) is that you might not *appear* manly enough. If female, that you might not *appear* feminine to the degree that men fall in their tracks on catching sight of you.

Because your Twelfth House is occupied by discriminating Virgo (Mercury ruler), you are more concerned with health, fastidiousness than one might guess. You are, on the surface, an artistic, sensitive individual who is not necessarily concerned with such matters as diet, health, weight reduction and so forth. But one of your secrets is that you are, that you are much concerned, and that you engage in secret exercises to correct real or imagined flaws.

Another secret is a firm belief that you possess extrasensory perception. You believe yourself to be psychic. Thus, many who regard you as forgetful or absent-minded are wrong. It is just that you feel you will "know" by induction; you feel the answers to questions are made available to you by some kind of universal mind, to which you are in tune. Yes, one of your major secrets is an unshakable belief in your mental powers. You have a high regard for your own intelligence. More important, you feel that your mind can transcend physical obstacles—such as distance—to perceive vital information. You believe in the *power of your mind.* Now, on the positive side, this is fine. But, on a negative level, you overlook details, feeling that, somehow, the answers will "come through." This, Libra, is not playing fair with yourself.

One of your major secrets, again, is a fear that you are not as healthy as you should be. Proper medical checkups, and following competent, professional instruction, should help overcome this tendency.

Here is another secret: you are often afraid to meet people you have admired at a distance. You feel the image of those persons—or your own—might collapse. Thus, Libra, you need more confidence, and you should add the ingredient of greater humor to your tremendous artistic sense. Actually, your hangups are few, but those you do have can be formidable.

You fear being alone. You have an intense need to share, to bring people together, to blend opposing views, to *synthesize*. Your secrets, in actuality, are basically constructive. You don't want to be hurt—this you share with many. But others can build resentment, can lash back, can cover themselves with protective shells. Not so you. You are exposed, open, receptive. You are idealistic enough to think the best of others, to want the best for them. Naturally, this makes you vulnerable.

You would rather be vulnerable than coarse. You would rather be hurt, if necessary, than unfeeling. It would seem, Libra, that you are capable of analyzing and that you know, in advance, when you are going to be emotionally stabbed. The key, then, is to avoid such encounters. But that is not you. The way you are constructed is such that you walk in and take the cold plunge, feeling that, somehow, you will get through and that the temperature will be bearable, if not pleasant. That's part of your Twelfth House, your secret self—a willingness to expose yourself to emotional danger.

In all, your secret self is mercurial, analytical; one of your secrets is that you feel your intuition will inform you of what is to occur. And your big secret is that you proceed, no matter what the consequences, having faith in the ultimate good.

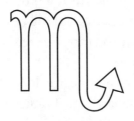

Scorpio
October 23 – November 21

Birthstones
Topaz and Malachite

Flower
Chrysanthemum

Numbers
2, 4, and 6

Color
Crimson

Parts of Body
Genitals

Cities
Dover, Liverpool, New Orleans, Washington, St. Johns, Baltimore, Santa Cruz, Cincinnati, Halifax, Olympia, Milwaukee, Newcastle, Anchorage, San Jose, Coos Bay, Stockton, Seattle

Countries
Algeria, Morocco, Norway, Tahiti

YOUR CHARACTER AND LIFE

Astrologers find your sign one of the most intriguing—
and controversial. Some are afraid of Scorpio. Some are
in awe. Others are puzzled. And still others are coolly analytical, claiming that you carry "secrets" which are almost
impossible to discern.

Whatever the truth may be, we do know that Scorpio is
the natural eighth zodiacal sign, belonging to the Water element, associated with Pluto. It is related to other people's
money, legacies, the occult, regeneration, the processes of
nature, and to tearing down and rebuilding.

Personally, for me, Scorpio has always been interesting and challenging: Scorpio stands for sex and repro-
duction; it is more powerful than Leo in this area. Scorpio is *there.* When a Scorpio is around, you know it and
so does everyone else. Scorpio leaves an imprint; Scorpio
is distinctive, intuitive, mysterious, glamorous.

Many think you are holding back when, if the truth be
known, you are reserved. Your nature is warm; where Libra
can be gentle and Leo can be affectionate, you can be passionate, and that's the key. You have to be reserved because,
once you let go, the cymbals sound and the colors are
bright. Your temper can rise, but usually that is a case of
righteous indignation. You can be jealous, but this is
because you have strong feelings. You're no cool cucum-
ber, make no mistake about that. When you feel, you
react. When you react, others know it. Vim and vigor—
plenty of *vigor*—that's you. Some fear you because they
sense you can sting, can retaliate when injured. You always
keep something in reserve, including your feelings. No

matter how much you "let go," there is something else—mysterious, magnetic, and hidden. It is there but it can be, for many, beyond comprehension. And the "many" includes *you.* You see, Scorpio, you cannot always delineate your own feelings, motives, or designs. You can be a mystery to yourself, but you know what love is all about because you feel.

You can rise to Olympian heights, like the eagle which symbolizes your sign; you can also sink to great depths, low as the scorpion, which also is your symbol. You are double, have a dual nature—not like Gemini, which is quick, mercurial—but a water-warm nature, rising and sinking, spunky, aggressive, and human enough to be outrageously secretive and jealous. That's you, Scorpio, inspiring prose which is strong, encouraging words which are contradictory and controversial. That's you, quick on the trigger, ready to give battle.

It is always a mistake to count you out. You come back. You are the phoenix, rising from its own ashes. You enjoy a good battle; it clears the emotional air. You are addicted to emotional high blood pressure. This means you get in and swing. You don't always land, but at least you create a breeze and put on a show. You will speak out of turn and be reprimanded. But even your apologies have life in them, a spirit of defiance. You can be aggressive even while saying you're sorry.

Plainly, you are capable of blowing your top. Conversely, you are also capable of helping your worst enemy, the competition, the foe. You love the feeling of being magnanimous; you're a poor loser because you openly feel that anyone who enjoys losing is a fool. You can be a gracious winner because, once the victory is attained, the other part of your nature surfaces: you lend a helping hand—or dollar.

You are forceful, direct (while maintaining an air of secrecy), at times obvious, while at other times subtle, even slinking—possessed of a creative drive which causes you to be restless, reckless and sexy.

Scorpio is a fixed sign, and you can be stubborn. No one pushes you around, not if you can help it. You're seldom helpless. You are intrigued with subjects many consider occult or forbidden.

Your sign signifies power, depth; it is the symbol of the detective, of hidden clues, of one who probes deep, who burrows until the right thing is found—who digs and digs until what is sought is finally discovered. Obviously, it's not wise to try to hide things from Scorpio.

You are dynamic, at times overbearing. Many cannot tolerate you, while others cannot do without you. Scorpio is sex and procreation—it is the eagle flying high, or the scorpion low on the ground. And you are either high or low, principled or irresponsible. You are joyous or miserable, tantalizing or crude. Clearly, you are not easy to understand because you cannot always fathom yourself. You can be grasping or giving, passionate or cold. But you make an *impression*.

Not many forget you. Some of your friendships last for years. Nor do you forget easily. You remember a slight; you savor a favor. Your arm can be long enough to lend a helping hand, or to put the finger on a suspect.

You are quite a person because you do react. You are not pale pink; you're bright crimson, and the water of your sign is either ice cold or boiling hot. That's what is important: it is there, with a temperature and a throb.

You are enthusiastic, bright, filled with the stuff of life. You battle for principles, but must learn to do a better job of evaluating. Too often, others lean on you. You exert effort, expend energy to aid those less than worthy.

I have often said in my talks to various groups and to astrologers themselves that if astrologers as a group have any prejudice, it is, unfortunately, often directed against your sign, Scorpio. There have been so many weird things written about you that, by this time, you could be excused for having either an inferiority or a superiority complex. The truth is that you are not inferior, nor are you necessarily superior. You are powerful, yet weak. You are strong, yet clinging. What you desire most is *understanding*. At times you shout at loved ones. This is an effort to shake them up, to make them come alive. You want to bring out the best in those close to you. But you don't always choose the most diplomatic methods.

Scorpio, your sign is a challenge. It represents the turmoil within us all. It represents the ambition contained in all of us. You are, in a way, all of us, because all of us can see some of our qualities, good and bad, reflected in you. You are capable, efficient, but along with these characteristics you also are emotional.

Your likes and dislikes tend to run to the extreme. There is little halfway about you—you are loyal, possessive, grasping; sometimes you grasp at straws in a desperate need to love and be loved. Scorpio is passionate, as we say. Yet Scorpio desires tenderness: a caress, a touch, a smile, or a gesture of understanding.

One of your outstanding characteristics is a willingness to *tear down* in order to rebuild. You are not awed by tradition. If tradition hampers progress, you will bypass it. Or, as we say, tear it down in order to get on with the stories, business at hand. You respect accomplishment, not stories about past glories. Now, Scorpio, this may be a workable theory where buildings, projects, special activities are concerned. But it is a different story where *people* enter the picture. You have an inward feeling that everything will turn out all right, or that the individuals involved will understand. When carried to extremes, you offend, you hurt; you push others away from you. And all the time, you are, inwardly at least, crying out for understanding. "Understand me! Know what I am doing and why I am doing it," that's what you say. Yet, one fine morning, you could wake up cold and alone, because the right, special person did not understand. So, Scorpio, it is obvious that you have to bend, to give a little, to make concessions—even sacrifices. Otherwise, not all of the progress, nor all of the gain, will mean a thing.

Listen, Scorpio: you play for high stakes: for inheritance, for eventual success, for greater love, for recognition—on your terms. But, Scorpio, the question is this: *just what are your terms?* That's the central point of the theme and the crux of the matter—your terms. You see, this requires maturity, as well as a tremendous degree of self-understanding, self-knowledge. And this leads us to yet another question: *Are you capable of such philosophical judgment, such maturity and wisdom?* If the answer is *yes*, then fine, all is well. We can follow your lead toward a goal of progress and enlightenment, toward material gain and comfort.

But, Scorpio, if the answer is negative—if you are not wise, mature, understanding—then there are problems. And the problems are of your own creation. You ask for simplicity and then create complications. You cry out for love and then shove it away, until it can meet your terms. You decry selfishness on the part of others, and then practice the opposite of what you preach. You are, you see, a virile individual—an individual in the extreme sense of the word; you are one of a kind. You are Scorpio and Pluto—you represent upheaval, life as opposed to the tranquility of peaceful sleep. That's why so many of us, including astrologers, are confused by your sign, and by you.

You are, if nothing else, forceful and resourceful. You are energetic, capable of rising to great heights, and of carrying others with you. But the others may have been perfectly contented to remain where they were. Now, Scorpio, this is something you find difficult to comprehend. And as a result you berate, you antagonize. Your voice becomes shrill as you insist that your wisdom, your terms are the best—if only people, especially those you love, would take heed, listen, absorb.

I have, perhaps, been a bit harsh in emphasizing some of your negative characteristics, and in stressing some of the abrasive elements of your makeup. But, Scorpio, I do this because, in etching a portrait of you that you will comprehend, I must be crystal clear. You can take it as well as give it. You would rather see the lines clearly than dimly. And perhaps all of us can envy you this striving for the truth—at any cost.

Listen, Scorpio: you are vital, ambitious. You would be the first to admit that indeed you do appreciate power.

Scorpio

You appreciate it for yourself, for others. You are a fierce competitor. And when the competition is over, you are sincerely puzzled if others are hurt or feel mistreated. You cringe at weakness but are the first to complain if others are made to suffer. You feel, in a sense, that all is well if you throw the punches. Somehow you rationalize your own strength, your power, your influence. Your blows can be understood, you feel. Others know the punches are thrown for a reason—that's what you tell yourself. But, when others do the punching, you are startled. You cry for justice. You will not tolerate a bully, you will not stand by while anyone is being bullied. But, at times, the very things you object to are the very things you do. In a sense you are the surgeon, but also the butcher. You are the power behind the throne. And you also are the revolutionary who topples the kingdom.

You can be so many things, Scorpio. But one thing you cannot be, and that is ignored. Some may disagree with you, but very few can ignore or forget you. You make a mark and leave an indelible impression. You are magnetic. You draw people, situations. You are, many times, a dilemma to yourself. You are kind to your enemies and harsh toward your friends. You can be aroused to great anger, and to sensitivity, kindness.

Your sign is associated with the reproductive organs. When you decide on something, you fix your view and stay on course—no matter what the consequences.

Many well-known people were born under Scorpio, including Dr. Jonas Salk, Burt Lancaster, Katharine Hepburn, Richard Burton, and Robert Ryan.

Scorpio

Incidentally, Scorpio Johnny Carson told me that his hobby is astronomy, but that he was also intrigued with astrology. Scorpions tend to be involved with the occult, with the hidden, with secrets, and with subjects that are considered underground, such as magic, palmistry, numerology, astrology. Johnny Carson once was a magician. He is a pretty good example of the positive Scorpio—one who is fixed, determined to achieve success, no matter how many setbacks.

As a Scorpio, you tend to become involved in secrets. But you never hide the fact that you are in a fight when you believe you are fighting for what is right. And listen: other people seem willing to trust you with secrets, with money. You are intrigued by law, and often are attracted to specializing in legacies, wills, in obtaining rights for one who lacks financial resources. You are forceful, direct, independent, aggressive. Your touch is magnetic, gentle but it is also physical and sexy. You take delight in calling the shots, forming policy, tightening or loosening the purse strings. The curtain goes up or down at your whim, or so you would desire. You have an unusual romantic nature your Fifth Solar House, related to romance is Pisces, ruled by Neptune. Thus, you build on illusion. You build illusions about the basics of life. At times you confuse illusion with fact, mistake wishful thinking for actualities.

At times, Scorpio, you seek one set of standards in others, but another, special set for yourself. You tend to give yourself credit for understanding, for being able to handle certain situations, but lack faith in others. This arouses envy, and causes some to doubt your sincerity.

Scorpio

Scorpio women have an abundance of extrasensory perception. They feel it when something of importance is
about to occur. Scorpio men are dynamic, aware of their
rights and abilities, and seem to become involved in lawsuits and difficulties over financial matters.

You are virile, intense, able to impress your will on
others. You are sexual, but can also seem oddly cool,
aloof, using sex as a weapon. Sometimes, however, the
weapon is turned against yourself. You punish yourself
for enjoying, berate yourself for not obtaining full satisfaction. The grass is greener, the horizons are brighter—
somewhere else. You are, as we say, difficult to comprehend. There are so many sides to your nature. You are
impressionable, but want to make an impression. You
are receptive, but want to give, state, dictate, form, and
complete policies.

You fight to protect what you own. But when the battle is over, and you have won, you might turn around and
give up what you fought so fiercely to protect. You are
mysterious, filled with contradictions. You are ingenious,
creative, capable of teaching great lessons. You are a true
friend and a dangerous enemy.

You uncover mysteries, secrets. You gain through inheritance; you save, accumulate. You prod and push and bring
out qualities we never knew we possessed, or that you were
capable of understanding.

Listen: whenever we think we know all there is to know
about you, you show us yet another side, not only of yourself, but of *ourselves.*

You are discerning. You penetrate outer layers and get
into inner areas *where we live.*

You are not fearful. You're not afraid of a fight although you never pretend to be a good loser. You are not afraid of ghosts, but probably believe in them. You inspire, delight, tantalize, frustrate, anger, give joy; you make life taste like garlic and salt, pepper and onions. That is to say, life with you is definite and not fleeting, wishy-washy, or tasteless. The taste is strong, and the aroma is one which gets the appetite going and causes emotions to rise. You believe in rising, not falling, and in succeeding, not failing.

You can cut through to the heart of matters. You can scrape and injure, but you can also heal and inspire. Listen: when all is said and done, you remain, basically, a mystery—and we all love a mystery—even if it scares us half to death!

THE SCORPIO LOVER

Now, to help all of us understand your sign to a greater degree, and to aid you toward more self-understanding I am going to present some special hints about your sign. First, here are some hints for men about women born under Scorpio: these women have an air of mystery, are often considered psychic. It is difficult to know them completely, for they change as circumstances demand. A man involved with a Scorpio woman may not always have an easy time—but he will know he's alive. Listen, men: don't seek a relationship with a Scorpio woman unless you are strong, willing to change your opinions, able to adjust, and have a basic respect for the opposite sex. The Scorpio woman is dynamic, explosive. She can lose her temper one minute and resemble a perfect angel the next. You are stepping on a merry-go-round when you begin courting a Scorpio woman. The pace may be dizzying, but you've asked for it so you have no right to complain. This woman—the Scorpio woman—can be fiercely loyal. She demands a great deal, but she also has much to give. She knows her way around when it comes to the practical aspects of living. This may puzzle you, for one day she can discuss finances like an expert, while the next day she is willing to follow a whim, a hunch. Obviously, she's not exactly easy to understand. Listen, men: I would say it's best to close your eyes to some of this, and enjoy the changes she is bound to make in your life. If you are the nervous or overly sensitive type—please seek another woman!

Now, let's present the women with some secret or special hints about men born under Scorpio: don't expect this man to say one thing and mean something else. He has a special gift for seeing through pretense, of knowing what others are really thinking, and what they are made of despite their statements or actions. He can perceive, delineate, render shrewd analyses of numerous people, situations, subjects. The Scorpio man is a tough one to fool. Scorpio men are physical, yet emotional. They require love in its poetic sense, yet can be animal-like. The Scorpio man can be brutal, but this does not necessarily stem from cruelty. Rather, it is brutality in a basic sense—brutal frankness, brutal honesty—nothing halfway. Let me give you one special hint. Don't try to reform this man. He knows what he wants and he usually has sound reasons for acting the way he does. If you want to lose him, start correcting his manners or his speech. If you want to keep him, try to understand and sympathize. The Scorpio man is forceful, direct, independent, and often aggressive. He is a man of action. If you want to impress him, you'll have to do more than talk or make promises. He wants results and, often, he demands that you prove your intentions. The Scorpio man can be jealous, very much so. He doesn't forget easily. Bear this in mind before you insult or ridicule him. He works hard and plays hard, and at times his appetites appear insatiable. If you really want him, you may have to meet and pass numerous tests. Once the examinations are over, however, you may feel the trouble was more than worthwhile.

YOUR RISING SIGN

All persons born under your sign are not exactly the same, although basic characteristics will hold. A horoscope, in actuality, is a map of the sky based on the time and place of birth. If you are aware of your birth time, here are some variations it may cause in your life and character:

Born between 4:00 and 6:00 A.M., your Rising Sign is apt to be the same as your Sun Sign, which is Scorpio, associated with Pluto. The double effect here tends to make you more serious, somber than is the average native of your sign. People depend on you, especially in financial matters. You seldom do anything halfway—it's all the way or nothing. More than others under your sign, you are intense. You concentrate on goals, challenges. You often create your own problems, especially where the opposite sex is concerned. You get involved. You relate to situations, individuals. You are able to discipline yourself. But there comes a time when you let go and break loose. Then conventions fall by the wayside. You are intuitive, perhaps psychic. Many claim you have healing powers. It is true that you can be of tremendous aid to others in both a psychological and physical sense.

Born between 6:00 and 8:00 A.M., your Ascendant is probably Sagittarius, ruled by Jupiter. This combines with your Pluto significator to lend a more philosophical bent to you than is possessed by the average native of your sign. You are also less practical. Your goals are not as solid as one might expect from members of your zodiacal group. You are more expansive; your desires are along lines which include deeper understanding of why people do what they do. This means you are intrigued with the psychological aspects of life. At times, you are too much the dreamer. You must learn to act on thoughts, ideas, to take more positive steps toward fulfilling wishes. You must also learn not to trust everyone who confronts you with a sob story.

Born between 8:00 and 10:00 A.M., your Rising Sign is apt to be Capricorn, associated with Saturn. This combines with your Pluto Solar significator to make you more versatile than the average native of your sign. You are able to achieve a number of objectives and you possess the wisdom to know when a change is necessary. This is very good for detecting financial trends. You are a father or mother image to many. And you can advise others on how to invest. Many owe you more than money. You're no angel but you are responsible and do respect the rights of others. You are one who probably does live up to the

Golden Rule. You would never deliberately do injury to another. Some consider you strait-laced . . . only because they have not troubled to know the real you.

Born between 10:00 A.M. and 12:00 noon, your Ascendant or Rising Sign is probably Aquarius, associated with Uranus. This combines with your Pluto Solar ruler to give you a sense of adventure. You are more apt to go to extremes than other members of your zodiacal group. You are idealistic and romantic; you feel that anything you can imagine can become a reality. You are inventive, exciting, and you can also be exasperating. Your interests are varied, with an accent on the occult, extrasensory perception, astrology, and psychology. You love luxury and can be extravagant. You desire to entertain and understand. You aid more people than you can imagine. Many speak well of you behind your back and argue with you when face to face. Strange but true!

Born between 12:00 noon and 2:00 P.M., your Rising Sign is apt to be Pisces, ruled by Neptune. This combines with your Pluto significator to make you even more intuitive than the average native of your sign. You are a natural teacher. You are able to fascinate , to hold an audience. You put your point across. You put yourself across—including footlights. Thus, you are attracted to drama, to the theater. You probably are no stranger to astrology and are concerned with the occult. You delve into unorthodox subjects—you attract people who are outside the conventional mold. You are sensitive. You are artistic. You are many things to many people. And you must do a better job of knowing who you ultimately are to be—to yourself.

Born between 2:00 and 4:00 P.M., your Rising Sign is apt to be Aries, ruled by Mars. This combines with your Pluto Solar significator to make you more direct than the average native of your sign. You are aware of rules but you can break them. You are aware of restrictions but can do away with them. You can, perhaps more so than the average member of your zodiacal group, tear down in order to rebuild. You can be pugnacious, independent, stubborn. But there usually is a purpose to what you do. Even while appearing to be careless, you know where each item is and why it has been so placed. You have a quick temper but you also are quick to forgive.

Born between 4:00 and 6:00 P.M., your Ascendant or Rising Sign is probably Taurus, associated with Venus. This combines with your Pluto Solar chart ruler to make you more determined—and obstinate—than the average native of your sign. You don't like to be told what to do. You will follow suggestions if made to think it was your idea in the first place. Once you get an idea, you go straight to the heart of the matter. You need to cultivate diplomacy. Many are attracted to you, especially the opposite sex. Your ego is the opposite of small; you have a high regard for yourself. You are sensuous. You can become a big financial success, but must learn to be more objective, more flexible.

Born between 6:00 and 8:00 P.M., your Ascendant is likely to be Gemini, associated with Mercury. This combines with your Pluto Solar ruler to make you more expressive than the average member of your zodiacal group. You have a gift for clarifying the complicated, for elucidating on complex subjects, and you can soothe troubled people in a manner to arouse the envy of professionals. You are more gregarious than is the average native of your sign. You attract people to you and many claim you are a born orator. Your ideas are unorthodox and your sense of humor comes to the fore during times of crisis. Music, the arts, medicine—these subjects attract you. Many who teach in these areas are likely to have your zodiacal pattern.

Born between 8:00 and 10:00 P.M., your Rising Sign is apt to be Cancer, ruled by the Moon. This combines with your Pluto significator to make you more impressionable than the average native of your sign. You are not only impressionable, you are apt to be psychic. You sense what people are feeling, thinking—what they are apt to do. You are fond of home life. You are loyal to your family. You are possessive and you are protective. You also are jealous. And you hate to let go of anything. Thus, you are possessive—of objects as well as people. You are a traditionalist, fascinated with antiques, history, your family tree. You want to belong to a group, family, nation; you want to be an integral part of your time and place. You want solidity and probably will be financially independent at a relatively early age.

Born between 10:00 P.M. and 12:00 midnight, your Ascendant is likely to be Leo, ruled by the Sun. This combines with your Pluto significator to make you more of a showman than the classic native of your sign. You love change, travel, variety; self-expression is essential to you. You have dramatic capabilities; your personal magnetism makes you popular with the opposite sex. You are creative and could write and act. You appreciate the talents of others. You make a wonderful audience because you react. Your views sometimes appear to be outrageous because this is your way of attracting attention. You are fond of children. You appreciate fine food, the good life. You have a tendency to overindulge because you seldom do anything on a small scale. For you, life is meant to be big and grand.

Born between 12:00 midnight and 2:00 A.M., your Rising Sign is likely to be Virgo, ruled by Mercury. This combines with your Pluto significator to make you more discerning than the average native of your sign. You possess a quality that is appealing. It has much to do with your wit and humor. Your laugh is disarming; it comes while you appear to be intense or preoccupied. Some say you have a soothing effect on people. Others say the opposite is true. You are puzzling to many because you change your mind about important subjects, but can be stubborn about apparently minor matters. You are apt to be an avid reader. You are analytical and a natural detective. You are never satisfied that something happened; you insist on knowing why it occurred. This quality can result in embarrassing moments and causes some to be uncomfortable in your presence.

Born between 2:00 and 4:00 A.M., your Rising Sign is apt to be Libra, ruled by Venus. This combines with your Pluto significator to make you more creative than the average native of your sign. You are a pioneer, capable of balancing the extraordinary with the ordinary; this results in a picture that reflects all of us in our unguarded moments. You reveal what is familiar, but always in a unique manner. You have a dramatic sense of originality; this enables others to see and understand. You are a natural pioneer, fond of nature and capable of imparting your enthusiasm. You are a conciliator. You can adjust to unusual conditions. You are basically a warm, giving individual and what you give most of is yourself.

SCORPIO FRIENDS AND PARTNERS

Scorpio is harmonious in relation to Virgo, Capricorn, Cancer, and Pisces. You are attracted to Taurus, but much in the manner that opposites attract each other. Scorpio is not favorably aspected to Leo or Aquarius, and is neutral in relation to Libra, Sagittarius, Aries, and Gemini.

With another Scorpio, there is apt to be a struggle for power. Both of you want to handle responsibility. You are attracted to each other. But you are possessive of each other and want to run the show each in his own way. There are problems, but they are not apt to be financial. Together, you can succeed in business but tend to bury the tender part of the relationship. You share power, money, and responsibility, but there could be a dearth of laughter. With another Scorpio, you aim toward success in a big way and could succeed in attaining major objectives.

SCORPIO CAREERS

Where career or occupation is concerned, you may be in the background, setting policy, but you demand credit. You may not be in front of the footlights, taking bows, but you want it known that you set the stage and created circumstances contributing to ultimate triumph. Many consult you and you are capable of aiding those who need help.

Scorpio

You are sympathetic, but you feel that ultimate help must come from the individual himself—and you don't hesitate to say so. You protect your organization, your employer; *you are jealous of your reputation.* This means you will go to almost any extent to protect prestige, to maintain standing. You are a fierce battler, a great ally, and a dangerous adversary.

Because of these qualities, you can be a fine executive. Your key word is strength. The following occupations are especially suitable: army officer, assayer, surgeon, dentist, detective, financial consultant, editorial director, and prison executive.

The Tenth House of a horoscope has to do with career, standing in the community, basic ambitions. That part of your chart is occupied by Leo, associated with the Sun. You find it necessary to be in a position to direct, to form policy, to produce a product that is in public demand.

Other careers in which you could find success include: aerodynamicist, loan company executive, bail bondsman, claims adjuster, insurance agent, X-ray expert, psychiatrist, paleontologist, and stock market research analyst.

You can keep a secret and you can uncover hidden factors. You may be behind the scenes but your presence is felt. There is an aura of authority which surrounds you. Money may not be your own, but you can raise it, collect it, bring together people who have it, and you can constructively use it. In plain words, you have a knack for knowing where money is and how to get your hands on it.

THE SCORPIO HAND

Some astrologers are proficient at guessing Sun signs; that is, they can look at an individual and perceive his, or her, zodiacal sign. This is no easy task—it requires experience, practice. The reason is that the Rising Sign (at the time and place of birth) affects personality and appearance, as does the sign the Moon occupied at birth. Yet, the place of the Sun is a strong indicator where character and appearance enter the picture.

Over the years, I have found that one significant key in this effort is the human hand. A person's hand often reveals whether that individual was born under a Fire, Earth, Air, or Water Sign.

You, Scorpio, were born under a Water Sign; Scorpio belongs to the Water element. The Water-type hand tends to be oval-shaped. It is more fleshy than average. Specifically, the Scorpio hand has a large Mount of Venus—that fleshy section found under the thumb. The hand is broad rather than long. The thumb itself can be rather short, club-like, indicating determination and obstinacy. The fingers tend to be thick. This is a soft hand, with the mounts or fleshy lumps under the fingers highly developed. Members of the Water signs, including Scorpio, seem almost psychic, able to perceive the thoughts of others.

The palm is fleshy; the lines of the hand deep, perhaps reddish in color. Like the character of Scorpio, the hand seems to have a definite purpose. It is fleshy, but not "wishy-washy."

There is plenty to this hand; it is ample. It is the opposite of the Air hand, which is long and delicate. The Scorpio hand is soft, but purposeful.

SCORPIO SECRETS

The horoscope, with its twelve angles or Houses, covers every area of life, including your secrets. The Twelfth House holds sway over secret fears, fantasies, undercover problems, all that is hidden or beneath the surface.

In your case, Libra occupies your Twelfth House; the Venus of Libra combines with your Pluto significator to show that your secret fear is that you will lag behind, that you will not be first. You do want to pioneer, much in the manner of Aries. You want to make an impression and your secret is that you want to do so with grace, class, and style. You envision yourself, in your fantasies, to be one who is in the vanguard where the arts and sciences are concerned. Your secrets include a fascination with law; you are, in your fantasies, leading a battle for justice. Very often this expresses itself in actuality; you become involved in lawsuits. You have a tendency to turn to law to protect your interests, to right real or imaginary wrongs.

Your secret is that you want to be the innovator; you would rather fail than imitate. You become furious when you feel your ideas are being confiscated. You have a fear of others taking over your plans and benefiting from your efforts without giving proper credit.

One of your secrets is your sensitivity. You attempt to cover your Venusian nature; you would rather be thought tough than sensitive, shrewd than aware. If the truth be known, you are a seeker of balance and harmony. If you had your way, you would be thought of as cantankerous, persistent, a rough rider with a big stick.

You want power and authority, but you also want to be loved. You want to win by acclamation, but you are willing to fight. You secretly desire to be the most popular person around, but you are willing to risk popularity for a principle.

Inwardly, you find a flower precious; outwardly, you would crush even the most delicate object which blocked a path to what you consider justice. You have the courage to declare war, but you yearn for peace. You have a deep-rooted feeling that you are misunderstood. You could be right. What you are in a true sense is very often camouflaged by outward appearances. Here a key is provided. You must learn to reveal more of what you are; you must let others see you, sense your true or inner self. When you do this, some of your secret desires will be fulfilled. You will be giving yourself a greater chance for finding love.

You are often surprised that others cannot, in fact, perceive what is you and what is camouflage. But that is essentially the way it is. Thus, you must rip away some of the secrecy of your nature; you must, in effect, make yourself vulnerable. In so doing, you will actually be making yourself strong. This may appear contradictory, but you will find that you'll gain a new lease on life. To be vulnerable, in this sense, is to lay yourself open for greater understanding, affection, and wisdom.

One major secret is a keen desire for unity, for joint effort, for true partnership—for a happy marriage. You want to be *accepted*. You want to be known for what you are, not for your outer covering, not for any facade you might present. However, you don't make it easy. Others tend to feel rebuffed at your not infrequent outbursts.

Your desire for love can be fulfilled. Your secret hopes and wishes can become realities.

The key, Scorpio, is not to keep them so secret.

Sagittarius
November 22 - December 21

Birthstone
Turquoise

Flowers
Holly and Narcissus

Numbers
3, 5, and 7

Color
Light Blue

Parts of Body
Hips and Thighs

Cities
Toledo, Cologne, Stuttgart,
Rotterdam, Nottingham,
Sheffield, Phoenix, Long
Beach, Denver, Acapulco

Countries
Australia, Hungary, Spain,
France (especially
Provence)

YOUR CHARACTER AND LIFE

Born under the natural ninth zodiacal sign, you are a philosopher; you analyze and deduct and explain. You piece together apparently unrelated parts and come up with a diagnosis. You enjoy the spotlight, especially when portraying a role. Because of this, you can be a teacher, an actor, one who demonstrates and illustrates. You are a visionary who tends to procrastinate. Your goals are the open road and the open mind. A clash of ideas is far more exciting to you than a clash of guns. You are a natural humanitarian, a reformer—when you tune in on a subject you are fervent.

Jupiter is associated with Sagittarius, and you are consequently expansive, drawn to subjects, such as medicine, that are designed to aid people. You are an analyst, a psychologist, a physician—you must, first of all, learn to heal yourself.

Your appeal is broad; you think of yourself not as belonging to a neighborhood but to the universe. You are artistic, creative, and ultrasensitive. Your life can be disrupted by emotional chaos, more so than is true of the average individual.

You enjoy being consulted. You are better at helping others than when it comes to aiding yourself. You are nobody's fool, but you are not above acting like one. Some people, especially of the opposite sex, can make you jump through hoops. Self-control and self-discipline are twin essentials, but they sometimes are lacking in you. You are good at advising, but you often neglect your own advice. Sagittarius is a Fire Sign, and you are impulsive. You believe in action, and this, very often, finds you traveling. The idea of going "on tour" appeals to you.

You want to communicate; it is something that drives you into politics, the theater, publishing. You leave your imprint on people, on your time; you want to influence your time through your thoughts, publications, writings, philosophy, ideas, actions.

You are expansive—and expensive—in that your principles are too high to enable you to settle for anything but the best: the best in quality, the best in agreements, the best in travel, the best in sportsmanship. You aim so high that, at times, you despair if your arrow fails to hit the right mark. It is then that you begin to retreat into a world of procrastination.

Your potential is great. But merely knowing that it is great is not enough. It is necessary to live up to the best in yourself. Otherwise, you brood; you begin berating yourself for "not doing enough."

Many Sagittarians are concerned with medicine. Sagittarians want to help others and often attract people to them with their problems. The key, however, is also to help yourself. Then you actually are in a better position to aid others. Remember to help yourself first. Turn dreams into realities. And you are capable of doing this, if you are determined and persistent.

A creative, artistic hobby is essential for your emotional well-being. You need such an outlet: sculpting, painting, writing, the theater. These are all part of your makeup, and it is not healthy to deny them.

You are not petty; you feel that you are above suspicion and you place people you love on the same level. At times you close your eyes to the obvious. This invites punishment. You know what's happening because few can pull the wool over your eyes. But you hide the facts from yourself, preferring an idyllic existence, preferring ideals to ideas, preferring to believe what makes you happy, no matter what the facts may be. In short, you don't want to be disturbed by actualities.

You were born under a Fire Sign—you are intense, romantic, and dramatic. In your love life, you tend to attract those who bully you in an emotional sense. You attract those who make you feel responsible for their welfare. As a matter of fact, Sagittarius, unless you are helping, advising, forming policies, you feel a lack, an emptiness. Sensing this, some people are only too willing to oblige. And, listen: you can create problems where no problems exist. By this, Sagittarius, I mean that you are so concerned with knowledge, education, idealism, that you tend to overlook the practical, the workable . . . and go seeking, when, in actuality, you already have what is required.

You are warm, but you tend to wander. You are in love with love. You flash with signs of talent, ardor, determination—but you also reveal a lack of staying power. Your key to greater success and happiness is the ability to *sustain* your drives, abilities, ambitions.

You appear easygoing, but could have ulcers. You, as we say, were born under the Fire Trinity; and you burn up on the inside while smiling on the outside. You are attractive to the opposite sex; this is fuel for your ego. You would rather be charming than rich. You would rather be considered sexy than scholarly. Your desire to be admired sometimes causes you to be considered something of a flirt. You tend to shift from one subject to another, one interest to another, one person to another. When you are loyal, you certainly are steadfast. But when you are through, or lose interest, you develop a convenient case of amnesia.

Travel can be an important part of your life. Your birth sign signifies long journeys, including journeys of the mind. You are concerned with the intellectual, with principles, education, knowledge. You are a natural humanitarian . . . a *humanist.* You are, as we said, attracted to long-distance travel and to communications, including writing, radio, television, recording, and publishing. You are attracted to the sea and to journeys via the sea. And perhaps because of this, you require an anchor. This often comes in the form of marriage—at times a marriage of convenience. You are basically conservative, yet you give the impression of being liberal, radical, able to break from standards, codes, accepted methods.

Although I have stated that you give the impression of being liberal, I would like to point out that you are a careful or a cautious liberal. You investigate first—act later—instead of the other way around.

Your greatest strength lies in your ability to be open-minded, to be open to various views, opinions. I would like to quote here from Vivian E. Robson, an authority on astrology and sex. He wrote much about you, Sagittarius, including this: *Perhaps the worst partner for a Sagittarian is a person of narrow and restricted views. A marriage of this sort . . . degenerates into sarcasm, bickering and general unhappiness, which, sometimes though not always, leads to separation.* I agree with Robson on this.

Listen, Sagittarius: I have stated that your great strength lies in being open-minded. I would add to this: your ability to accept, to be expansive, to be expressive. It is, Sagittarius, better for you to accept than to reject. As a matter of fact, you're never happy when suspicious. You want to accept, to look for and to expect the best.

It is better for you to accept than to reject, better to love than to hate, better to say *yes* than to disapprove. You need an outlet for your idealism. This leads to a search. You search for causes, for people to help. You become involved in the medical and mental problems of others. That's when you're happiest, when you're most fulfilled—when you help others, you are happier than when others aid you. You feel you are in a vacuum if there is nothing to expound, to gather around, to become enthusiastic over. If you don't have a cause, you tend to shrivel, to become petty, to express the negative rather than the positive side of your character.

Your sign is fascinating. Your humor is robust. William Buckley was born a Sagittarian. So were Frank Sinatra, Van Heflin, J. Paul Getty, Jane Fonda, Sammy Davis, Jr., and Eli Wallach.

Your humor is more than robust; it is often coupled with irony. You can be patient to the point of exasperation. At times, your patience seems to be laziness, an acceptance of the status quo, an inability to do anything but move in circles. Sometimes the movement is vigorous, but nevertheless, it can be in the form of a circle. That, Sagittarius, is when you don't have a cause, a goal, a problem to overcome for someone else. It is obvious that you are better at helping others than at aiding yourself. You are versatile, artistic, capable of expressing yourself well enough to be an actor, actress, painter, or designer. You are fascinated with the idea of communicating your thoughts to others, and thus would be attracted also to the fields of writing and publishing.

Listen, Sagittarius: I must include among the things I say about you that you are a natural teacher, an explainer, a delineator. You piece together bits of information and come up with the complete story, not so much as a detective might do, but as one does who wants to explain, to clarify. You mold yourself into a situation, a character, for the specific purpose of explaining, of expressing. You are an actor, writer, teacher, publisher, reporter, news analyst, or investigator of some sort. You are, in short, an explainer. You are, as one might expect, excellent at relating anecdotes. You appear to be a good listener. But, often, while listening, your mind is far away, thinking of answers, explanations. One must hit you hard to get your attention, to grab and really hold it. It isn't easy to reach you, to touch you—but once you are caught, you tend to be loyal.

You can be disarming because you give the impression of completely trusting others. In turn, this inspires others to trust you, to have faith, to confide. Very seldom do others realize that you are embarked on a journey of the mind, appearing to be here, with us, while actually you are dreaming away, being a visionary, a mystic, a creator.

As a Sagittarian, you are very considerate. At times, those close to you wish you wouldn't be so considerate, so aware of the feelings of others. They would like to see you please yourself, like to see you forget duties, obligations to the point of losing yourself in emotion. Of course, this would be negative if carried to extremes. But the point is, Sagittarius, that you tend to be too aware, sometimes to the degree of being calculating where the emotions of others are concerned. You want to please, to satisfy, to help; if carried too far, this causes resentment on the part of those you try to help. They want to return the favor—they want you to let your hair down.

Your sign is associated with the hips and thighs in particular, but with all the tendons of the muscular system in general. Your health is usually good, but you are subject to attacks of nervous disorders when you neglect your diet, your need for proper rest. Your recuperative powers, however, are marvelous.

Sagittarius, you are proud, sensitive. Your intuition is honed to razor-sharpness. Many are convinced that you possess extrasensory perception.

You are, Sagittarius, a bundle of contradictions. You fight prejudice, but adore your own private convictions. In your mind, your personal prejudices are transformed into noble convictions. That's why, Sagittarius, it is so difficult to argue with you. At times your mind is made up and you don't want it cluttered by more facts.

Here are some additional qualities that are special where you are concerned: you want to be a great lover, but are disdainful of those who exhibit qualities associated with lust. You want to be expansive, but chide those who exhibit ambition. You want success, but ridicule those who obtain it without adhering to your idea of idealism. You want freedom, but tie yourself down to menial tasks in order, one day, to be free. You are an expert at defeating your own purpose, but continue to hope for the best. You are,

Sagittarius, an optimist, but also a cynic. You are congenial, a fine storyteller, but you become bored with others who, in your opinion, talk too much.

Listen: you are many things to many people. And the lesson to learn is that what you are *to yourself* is what counts. Until you learn it, you are likely to cast about, tasting various philosophies, people, even cults.

You are capable of inspiring profound admiration, but you set goals so high that you have a difficult time living up to expectations. You are a philosopher who lives within, yet pays entirely too much attention to the outside, to what others think and to how others react to your efforts and actions.

Let me repeat the fact that you do require a goal. It could be an overseas journey, a book you are going to read or write, a person you are going to love or oppose, an ambition, a *future.* Your great weakness is transforming this future goal into past memories. That is, on the negative side, the goal becomes mere speculation and you fall back on past achievements or on *what might have been.* You can be a bit of a bore when you rely on scrapbooks, clippings, shopworn anecdotes. Your greatest strength is in learning from experience, in absorbing knowledge from actual contacts with people.

Listen, Sagittarius: throw away some of the theories, the textbooks, the prejudices—throw them overboard and start now to form your own conclusions based on experience, direct contacts, from touching and being touched. Living dangerously is better than not living at all; that, Sagittarius, should be your credo and, very likely, it is. You are a natural explorer—you delve into hidden crevices—you dare the unknown and often bring the unknown closer, so that we all can examine and benefit from greater knowledge.

You are an individual who possesses much pride. But pride often becomes your worst enemy. It keeps you from admitting a mistake, keeps you from crying when wounded. It keeps you laughing when, for the benefit of your emotional well-being, you should be crying.

You can, when you lose control, go to extremes—in eating, drinking, affairs of the heart. You can also become a health bug, or an outdoor type who cares more for animals than for people.

You are an intellectual with a keen sense of adventure. You are, Sagittarius, a unique individual who attracts great friends but who is capable of creating envy and enemies.

Listen: you must learn to revere differences rather than to fear them. Being different is not to be equated with being inferior. And stop feeling you must constantly improve and prove yourself. A member of the opposite sex is a person, an individual, not necessarily a challenge. You don't have to win, to conquer. Appreciate what you have and what you are. Then life becomes smooth rather than rocky, happy rather than conflict-filled.

What you are and what you express don't always add up to the same thing. Check your figures. Get them right. Let us see the real you, because that's what we desire. It is *you* we want, not an imitation, not a book, a character, a creation. *You!*

The real you is frank, impulsive, restless, candid, an individual in the true sense, with an abundance of intellectual curiosity. You are happiest close to nature, to the healing arts, to learning, to progress. You are most pleased when reading, writing, creating, knowing that someone you love is close at hand and that all is right with the world—or soon will be with your help.

You are dynamic; your ego needs nursing. Like Leo, you can be susceptible to flattery. You are special and often deserve praise. But a calculating individual, knowing of this susceptibility, could take unfair advantage. Realize this and mix practicality with your idealism.

You can be kind and generous. But when pushed too far, you can also be vindictive. You are generous and, at times, extravagant. You want life to be grand, glorious, and you will break the rules to lay treasures at the feet of those you love. You are special, too special for the taste of some.

Listen: the key is to be what you are and not try to create an illusion of someone else. If that lesson seeps through, then you will have gained something of tremendous value.

Learn to accept as well as to give. Throw off that shell which causes you to view yourself as the generous father (or mother) figure. Humble yourself to the point of accepting. This will make those around you much happier. If you give, and give, guilt feelings boil up in others. If you accept, others feel needed and, in turn, will make you feel that you are indeed fulfilling a paramount role.

The Sagittarius Lover

I believe that secret or special hints for men and women about your sign are especially important where Sagittarius is concerned. Here are some special tips for women about men born under your sign, Sagittarius.

Sagittarius

This is for women only: the Sagittarius man will make you know you are a woman, and he'll also make you live up to being a woman. The Sagittarius man dislikes petty people. He can help you grow and he will expect you to be a big person. Otherwise, his initial attraction could turn to revulsion. During a time of emergency, he thinks quickly, he acts; he acts in a sure, decisive manner when there is trouble.

Sagittarius men want to learn by reading, doing, experimenting, questioning, traveling, writing, examining, probing. If the kind of life you want is a sit-still kind, then obviously, the Sagittarius man is not for you. But if what I have described appeals to you, then there is the way to catch him. You catch the Sagittarius man with color, charm, wit. You intrigue him by asking fantastic questions. You cause him to lose interest by being too conventional in your outlook, ambitions, questions. The Sagittarius man wants companionship, more so than do others. He wants to share his experiences, adventures. Stick to your views, but spotlight your individuality. He may appear to rebel, but the one quality he admires in a woman, above all else, is independence. Be challenging. Be original, independent, and ask plenty of questions—and you'll catch and keep the Sagittarius man.

Now, let's turn to the other side of the coin. This is for men only about women born under Sagittarius.

The Sagittarius woman is an idealist. Honesty and frankness are her key words. Her decisions are swift. Impulsive actions, at times, get her into difficulty. If you want this woman, stress integrity. Respect comes first—then love grows, as far as the Sagittarius woman is concerned. She is proud, refined, sensitive. Don't attempt to pressure her.

Let her decide, let her make up her own mind. She has a fiery temperament, and if you attempt to fight her you could have quite a battle on your hands. A Sagittarius woman is exciting, yet gives the impression of being shy. She presents a challenge—she brings out the best in you. She is something special, and worth any trouble you have to endure to win her.

Let me stress that it is important to be honest, to be forthright, to state your intentions to the Sagittarius woman. Don't attempt cover-ups, false promises, statements. If you are frank, you are most likely to succeed with this woman. Another hint about the Sagittarius woman: *she is drawn to men who are kind to animals.* She is attracted to men who talk about the outdoors, who appreciate nature and the wonders of natural beauty. Now, armed with these special hints, you should be able to capture the heart of the Sagittarius woman!

YOUR RISING SIGN

All persons born under your sign are not exactly the same, although basic characteristics will hold. A horoscope, in actuality, is a map of the sky based on the time and place of birth. If you are aware of your birth time, here are some variations it may cause in your life and character:

Born between 4:00 and 6:00 A.M., your Rising Sign is likely to be the same as your Sun Sign, which is Sagittarius, associated with Jupiter. This intensifies the characteristics described in this section. You are generous, idealistic to a fault, more concerned than the average member of your sign with religion and philosophy. Various cultures fascinate you.

Foreign lands intrigue you. People who practice unusual customs draw you. So does education and so do languages. You learn the customs of people who practice what appear to be strange rituals. You are frank and, at times, outspoken to a point that some consider offensive. But that's you: a battler against prejudice, a fighter for justice, an individual with an insatiable appetite for knowledge. You love life, and travel is one aspect of living that is especially dear. You are extravagant, so concerned with the big pictures that you tend to be absent-minded about apparent minor affairs. You want to be surrounded by people you love, by art and beauty. You want life to be beautiful, and when it is not you are akin to a child who has had his candy taken away.

Born between 6:00 and 8:00 A.M., your Rising Sign is likely to be Capricorn, ruled by Saturn. This combines with your Jupiter Solar significator to make you more intuitive than the average native of your sign. You tend to be slightly withdrawn, serious of purpose, and more frugal than the classic member of your sign, too. Your sense of responsibility is sharply honed. You are ambitious and have a good business sense. You are capable of transforming talents into profits. You are patient; you wait for results. Once you decide to achieve a goal, you are persistent: you strive and wait, somehow knowing that the result will be in accordance with your image of it. You weigh, judge, balance; you can size up people and situations. You know the score, and how to utilize popular terminology; you know where it's at. You can be in the thick of excitement and still be capable of seeing beyond the immediate.

Born between 8:00 and 10:00 A.M., your Rising Sign or Ascendant is probably Aquarius, associated with the planet Uranus—this combines with your Jupiter Solar significator to make you more curious about unorthodox subjects than the average native of your sign. Your idealism is intensified. Your ability to perceive future trends is heightened. You are an exciting individual. You are fond of change, travel, variety; you are akin to a detective in your ability to piece together bits of information. You usually get the complete picture while your colleagues are pondering, wondering, still guessing. You have a knack for meeting influential people. You are helped through your social contacts. Aviation intrigues you and you probably enjoy flying. You are concerned with people and their general welfare. Astrology would make a wonderful avocation, if not profession, for you. You help others in realizing their potential. You crave adventure and you are usually on the side of the unorthodox. At times, you go to extremes. Once you gain a greater sense of time you will be a world-beater.

Born between 10:00 A.M. and 12:00 noon, your Ascendant is likely to be Pisces, ruled by Neptune. This combines with your Jupiter Solar significator to bring you into contact with people who are innovators. You possess a pioneering spirit. You are sensitive. You learn quickly. You are intuitive and often wake up with answers which elude most people. You are creative, altruistic, and seem able to perceive the future. You fool people because some think of you as a dreamer. But your dreams can be fulfilled, and often become realities. You adapt to changing conditions and you inspire people to follow your dictates. You do this in a subtle manner. You don't rush, force, or push. Rather, you win your way, often with the backing of, say, a club, group, or organization. You would make a fine fundraiser. You can make others realize that what you advocate is worthwhile.

Born between 12:00 noon and 2:00 P.M., your Rising Sign is likely to be Aries, associated with the planet Mars. This combines with your Jupiter Solar ruler to make you more versatile than the average native of your sign. You are independent in thought, action; you lead rather than follow. Some think you are domineering. In actuality, you know what you want and you go after it. It might pay you to be a bit more subtle. You are outspoken, at times pugnacious, very energetic, and capable of overcoming odds. You can be counted on to do the unexpected; your pattern is a combination of that of a dreamer and a man of action. You work and play with gusto; your sense of humor is a great asset. You can make people laugh when they think they are going to cry. You make friends quickly. You are direct, frank, and when you perceive an injustice you fight to rectify it. At times you become impatient. For you, this is more dangerous than it is for the average person. Impatience can lead you to impulsive actions—when this occurs you can defeat major purposes.

Born between 2:00 and 4:00 P.M., your Rising Sign is likely to be Taurus, ruled by Venus. This combines with your Jupiter Solar significator to make you more appealing than the average native of your sign. This means you can be diplomatic; you can be patient as well as persistent. You seem to be lucky where money is concerned. You could have the fabled Midas touch. You also have a tendency to indulge yourself. You love luxury and spend almost as much as you earn. Art objects intrigue you. For you, beauty is essential, and so is comfort. You are very attractive to the opposite sex. Some complain that you are too accustomed to getting your own way. But this is because you have no guilt feelings about enjoying yourself. Those who complain actually envy you. You can spot a bargain a mile away, but will never substitute this for quality. You could successfully connect with an overseas operation or business you sense what is good for importing and exporting.

Born between 4:00 and 6:00 P.M., your Ascendant is likely to be Gemini, associated with Mercury. This combines with your Jupiter Solar ruler to make you more sure, positive, and confident than the classic native of your sign. You are perceptive. You gain through reading, writing; learning satisfies your inner desires. Your mind is active, even when you're at rest. Your curiosity drives you; you are restless, constantly on the go. You are a natural flirt. A number of people may misunderstand this and accuse you of something more serious; you *seem* able to love more than one person at a time. But, in reality, you are testing, probing, experimenting, trying to find who is most suitable for you. At times, you are exasperating, especially to yourself. Despite an air of devil-may-care, you handle responsibility well. You dig in and accomplish things. Your mental processes churn; you are usually one or more steps ahead of your competition. You are concerned with motives and are not above a scheme or two of your own.

Born between 6:00 and 8:00 P.M., your Rising Sign is likely to be Cancer, ruled by the Moon. This combines with your Jupiter Solar significator to make you sensitive and capable of building on a solid base. You can be overly possessive, especially where people you love are concerned. You are a romantic. You would build a castle to give pleasure to someone you love. You are intuitive enough to make major adjustments when new conditions present themselves. You enjoy adulation and constantly seek approval. But you are no fool where flattery is concerned. You like to get promises in writing—and you usually succeed in so doing. Some may say you are grasping. But these people are usually those who have witnessed your ability to take advantage of an opportunity that they permitted to slip away. You are fortunate in that your efforts are rewarded in a material sense. However, your own family does not always share in the applause. You can be taken for granted by those who mean the most to you.

Born between 8:00 and 10:00 P.M., your Ascendant is probably Leo, ruled by the Sun. This combines with your Jupiter Solar chart significator to provide you with more showmanship than is possessed by the average native of your sign. You are fond of the spotlight, and often defy conventions. You learn the rules but also break them. You love challenge. You make your mark when most people think you are finished. You are inwardly strong, even when you appear to lack seriousness of purpose. You are extravagant, but you mainly want to provide pleasure for others. You are fiery, at times temperamental. You desire perfection, but are shrewd enough to know that you must be patient. Your persistence at times is transformed into obstinacy. You are not easy to live with, but those who care wouldn't want to live without you. You are romantic, dramatic, and affectionate. Life without love is no life for you. You can be hurt, but it is often you who create intolerable situations. Less impulsiveness and more steady planning can bring constructive changes.

Born between 10:00 P.M. and 12:00 midnight, your Rising Sign is apt to be Virgo, associated with Mercury. This combines with your Jupiter Solar significator to make you more aware of the future than the average native of your sign. You are perceptive, capable of taking the pulse of the public. You are concerned with social justice. You draw people to you with their problems. You can devote yourself to a cause. You can gain wide recognition. You can become famous. You are never likely to be satisfied with conditions as they are—you want change, justice, perfection, the kind of world in which all can prosper emotionally and otherwise. You are an idealist. But you also have ideas that can overcome the odds and accomplish what appears to be impossible. Your potential is limitless. But you do have a tendency to carry burdens not rightly your own. These can weigh you down. Learn not to let others take advantage of you. Be considerate without foolishly giving of your time and energy.

Born between 12:00 midnight and 2:00 A.M., your Rising Sign is likely to be Libra, ruled by Venus. This combines with your Jupiter Solar significator to make you more aware of justice and balance than the average native of your sign. You need love; you crave it. You fight for what you consider to be right. But you need someone by your side, on your side; one who understands and comprehends your goals and aspirations. You can be fortunate in both love and money; this depends on your judgment, maturity. A balance between emotional and logical reactions is a necessity for you. You are attracted to law. You can sway and persuade. You can delineate subtle nuances of character. And you can appreciate creative, artistic endeavors. Your selections of clothes, paintings, household objects are much admired. You are attractive to the opposite sex. But you often wear your heart on your sleeve—make an attempt to discipline your emotions a bit more. Learn to protect yourself further.

Born between 2:00 and 4:00 A.M., your Rising Sign or Ascendant is apt to be Scorpio, associated with Pluto. This combines with your Jupiter Solar significator to make you more intense than the average native of your sign. You are introspective. You need an outlet for your emotions. But you often keep your feelings to yourself. You can be a victim of self-deception. You know what is right, but you tend to see people and situations as if you were looking through rose-colored glasses. You are almost psychic; you can detect the moods of others. You are considered sexy. You are dynamic, but what you really feel is often kept under wraps. You are fascinated with the occult, the hidden. You make things difficult for yourself because you never choose the obvious. You prefer to overcome obstacles. You want to do good works and are attracted to law and religion. Learn to be more moderate where your appetites are concerned. You can go to extremes when you let yourself go. You are ultimately in control—when you make an effort. Do so, and you enhance chances for success and happiness.

SAGITTARIUS FRIENDS AND PARTNERS

Sagittarius is harmonious in relation to Libra, Aquarius, Leo, and Aries. Your sign is not well-aspected to Pisces, Virgo, or Gemini and is considered neutral to Scorpio, Capricorn, Taurus, and Cancer.

With another Sagittarian, you have a desire for home, domesticity, but you also want a relationship free of flaws. You idealize and leave yourself open to disillusionment. There is basic understanding. You see many of your own traits, but usually the less desirable ones. This causes you to criticize because, perhaps subconsciously, you become aware of your own shortcomings. The relationship can be permanent, but not trouble-free. The success of it depends on the maturity of the Sagittarians involved. Your wandering days could be over with another Sagittarian; you could find a home.

SAGITTARIUS CAREERS

Travel, law, and publishing are occupations for which you have an affinity. You are seldom happy if restricted, tied down, burdened with details. You have flair and style, and you need an outlet for self-expression.

The Tenth House of a horoscope has to do, among other things, with career, ambitions, prestige, standing in a community, and general success through occupational efforts. The Tenth Sector of your Solar horoscope is Virgo, associated with the planet Mercury. With Virgo on the cusp, of your Tenth Sector, the success indicators in writing and publishing—and in creating special services—are heightened.

You could succeed as a publisher, in fields where foresight is required. You are capable of knowing what will be "in" next week, next month, next year. You are not married to tradition; you are willing to expand, to break down barriers. You would be particularly happy—and successful—as part of the travel or transportation industry. You make others feel at home no matter how far they may be from where they live.

Other occupations which harmonize with your sign include: attorney, clergyman, editor, copy writer, woolen merchant, sporting goods manufacturer, public relations specialist, broadcasting engineer, radar technician, and physical education instructor.

You are constantly involved in affairs concerned with public welfare. You are a firm believer in the right of self-expression. And when you become a part of a drive, or an industry aimed at serving the needs of people, you do so in a full spirit, happy only when you feel the job has been accomplished.

The open road of a theatrical tour . . . of a luxury cruise, which sees you as a recreation or cruise director . . . these and the careers already noted are indicated by your Sun Sign, and your Tenth House.

THE SAGITTARIUS HAND

Some astrologers are proficient at guessing Sun signs; that is, they can look at an individual and perceive his, or her, zodiacal sign. This is no easy task—it requires experience, practice. The reason is that the Rising Sign (at the time and place of birth) affects personality and appearance, as does the sign the Moon occupied at birth. Yet, the place of the Sun is a strong indicator where character and appearance enter the picture.

Over the years, I have found that one significant key in this effort is the human hand. A person's hand often reveals whether that individual was born under a Fire, Earth, Air, or Water Sign.

You, Sagittarius, were born under a Fire Sign; Sagittarius belongs to the Fire element. The Fire-type hand is comparatively small, with the palm larger than the combined fingers; the hand is conic or cone-shaped—broad at the base and tapering toward the fingers. Fire Sign natives can often be identified by high foreheads, too; there is a tendency for the hair to move back, giving the Fire Sign member an intellectual appearance.

Some natives of the Fire signs, particularly Aries, tend to squint and many wear glasses. The Fire signs are Aries, Leo, and Sagittarius. Your hand, Sagittarius, will very likely be larger than the hands of Leo and Aries. But your hand will be smaller than those of the Earth signs.

Since you are active intellectually, your hand will probably be well-lined, with a sloping, well-marked head line, that line which emerges across the hand from between (about middle distance) the forefinger and thumb.

SAGITTARIUS SECRETS

The horoscope, with its twelve angles or Houses, covers every area of life, including your secrets. The Twelfth House holds sway over secret fears, fantasies, undercover problems, all that is hidden or beneath the surface.

In your case, Scorpio occupies your Twelfth House; the Jupiter of your sign combines with the Pluto of Scorpio to reveal that your secret fear is that you might be fooling yourself about specific talents, abilities, motives, and goals.

One of your secrets is the degree of intensity which is part of your makeup. You tend to keep it pretty well hidden. But the fact is that you are not only intellectual but deeply concerned with what many term "the occult." That is to say, the hidden; you believe in your hunches, intuition, inner feelings. You do not, of course, always make this apparent. Many would be surprised to know that one of your major secrets is an intense desire to know completely, and understand, the inner workings of others. This, in some ways, stems from a fear of being deceived, especially where the opposite sex is concerned.

Another hidden part of you is your mysticism. Much of your knowledge is subjective rather than objective. And you are especially subjective in connection with affairs of the heart, with the opposite sex. You leave yourself open to punishment by "refusing to be confused by the facts." One of your secrets, too, is an extreme tendency to see people as you wish they might be. This, to a large extent, negates an objective view. It also leaves you open to the very thing you fear—deception, even betrayal.

Your main secret, in effect, is that you believe what you want to believe. Another secret is that you do know better. You probe deep; you are a natural analyst. You instinctively size up people and situations. But, once your emotions are involved, it is usually good-bye to logic. Seeing this in cold print might help correct the situation. It is hoped that this will be the case, so you won't waste some of yourself chasing rainbows.

Another secret is that you want to be powerful; you have a desire to make definite impressions. You want to be considered sexy as well as creative, and you want money—on your own terms. This is a secret because it is almost the opposite of the impression most people have of you.

You tend to doubt existing structures. This applies to those who affect you, where you live, and to society in general. You want to rebuild on your own grand scale. You are idealistic in a special sense: in the sense of feeling that whatever exists can be improved, that people can always be helped, that the world can live in bountiful peace. That part of you is not so much a secret. But it is less known that you inwardly feel much that exists now has to be torn down and replaced, and that you have the vision, the know-how to accomplish this feat.

Another secret is a distinct tendency to brood. This is mentioned here in an effort to make you realize the senselessness of worrying or ruminating over something you can do nothing about.

Some of these secrets of yours can be destructive if they get out of control. On the constructive side, most of your secrets can help you to fulfill your ideals. Your secrets represent solid ambition and goals that are worthwhile. You should not be discouraged or disillusioned if some people you count on turn out to have feet of clay. Your own sense of balance is important, not what others think of you. You, personally, are capable, energetic, idealistic, and a force for the good. Stop berating yourself for not being able to accomplish the impossible overnight.

Capricorn
December 22 - January 19

Birthstones
White Onyx, Moonstone,
and Garnet

Flower
Carnation

Numbers
2, 8, and 9

Colors
Black and Green

Parts of Body
Knees

Cities
Oxford, Brussels, Contance,
Birmingham, Bridgeport,
Chicago, Boston, Baltimore,
Providence, Montreal, Port
Said, Milwaukee

Countries
India, Afghanistan, Greece,
Albania, Bulgaria, Mexico

Your Character and Life

Your sign is one of the most misunderstood, having this dubious honor in common with Scorpio. That's why you often have to "play with time"; you have to bide your time. You have to play the waiting game. You know that what you say, do, think, create—takes time to "catch on."

There is an aura of the reserved about you. And unless others take the time to penetrate it, there is little understanding from them. Capricorn is associated with one of the most respected—and feared—planets. That planet is Saturn, symbolizing power, responsibility, restriction, pressure, and discipline. It also symbolizes eventual recognition. Capricorn is the natural tenth zodiacal sign, related to career, standing in the community, ambition, and success.

Listen: you have an *affinity with time.* You understand it. You can cope with it. *You can wait and win.*

My colleague, Carl Payne Tobey, is refreshingly frank and puts his finger on many Capricorn qualities which are "there," whether or not they surface or become visible. The point is that there are other sides to you—deep feelings into which you often take refuge. You can become insulated, seeking protection in an emotional shell. This is not always attractive, nor is it wise. To express yourself is a necessity; to give of yourself is also important. To do these things, you must cast aside the shell; you must allow yourself to be vulnerable. In so doing, you will also become vulnerable to joy, as well as to possible pain.

Some claim you are cold. But the fact is that you were born under a sign that means you can sizzle with sex, can be drenched with desire; the need for warmth makes you draw love, makes you reach out, makes you generally a rival with anyone where love and passion are concerned.

Listen: I said you could be cold with desire. This is not a contradiction, not the way I mean it. Many people can have love withdrawn, and yet find balance, find warmth in other endeavors. But, with love withdrawn, with love absent, with love not yet discovered—there is, for you, no substitute, no replacement. In a very real sense, you can become cold with desire. You can become physically and emotionally ill from the absence of love, just as some can become cold and ill through lack of proper attire or shelter during inclement weather. The inclement weather, for you, occurs in the absence of emotional fulfillment, through the absence of a loving partner.

Saturn (the planet associated with Capricorn) symbolizes patience, discipline, these qualities do not make you easy to know. You don't always know yourself. You can act one way, feel another—you possess dignity and this is often misinterpreted. You can appear aloof, when you merely are covering your emotions in an effort to protect yourself.

When you do let go . . . it is all the way. That's why you are reluctant to open up on all occasions. You save yourself, you conserve, you try to pick and choose. You don't always choose correctly. That's obvious when you review your personal background, experiences. But, nevertheless, you are not cold, certainly not indifferent: you are, in actual fact, quite sensitive, although it doesn't "show," not (for example) like sensitivity "shows" in a Libran or a Piscean.

Listen, Capricorn: at times you give the impression of either being indifferent, or completely physical. You change, very often you do things, or appear to do things, merely for shock value. Which means that what you do depends, very often, on what reaction you feel will be forthcoming. And the reaction you seek is not always approval: it could be shock, disapproval, surprise, or—on the other side of the coin—complete approval. You can be chameleon-like: subject to change, apt to run hot and cold. You are capricious: your likes and dislikes vary. You want to see how others will respond, how they will take you. All of this, as one might imagine, does lead to a variety of experiences, and emotional ups and downs.

Your emotions are powerful—seldom halfway. All the way or nothing. You stick. You suffer. You go down more than three times and when it appears surely you are down and out—up you bob again. You haven't drowned, as many thought. Instead, you are up, leaving the water, walking away, snorting, butting, shaking off the side effects of yet another experience, perhaps bizarre, perhaps sad, maybe hilarious.

By now it is apparent that your sign, the tenth, the top sign . . . on top of the horoscope . . . a cardinal sign . . . having to do with occupation, career, leadership, profession . . . indicates that you are tough, resilient, capable of plodding to victory, of suffering, of carrying burdens, of being docile or pugnacious, whichever need be at the moment. And this could involve any length of time required for your project.

The project could be a book, a love affair, a lifetime. You are, Capricorn, metaphysically inclined because you are so closely aligned to time. Attuned to time might be a better way of putting it. Time, for you, has its own personality—every moment of time is different—each time is different. You are not easy to understand because you attempt to comprehend the universe. Often your husband or wife, someone you love, or friends will rise up and shout, "How about understanding me—just me—plain little old me . . . instead of the world, the universe, everyone else—how about me?"

And there is a point to that plea. For, Capricorn, until you can bring your perception, your powers to bear on the immediate, the real as opposed to the symbol, then you are losing much, permitting the world to go by without really partaking of it. You can't be truly happy unless you do partake, unless you participate for, among other things, you are worldly. Saturn, your planetary significator, is both spiritual and worldly; it requires and demands discipline. But it also offers rewards. You are to live now, here on earth. You are earthy, practical, real enough to love and yet . . . yet your eyes look out, to the future, the distance, the ideal, the utopia; and you are sure you will sail that journey one day, take that trip which brings you to a kind of personal Shangri-La.

Many celebrities were born under your sign, including writer Henry Miller, Ava Gardner, Ray Milland, Marlene Dietrich, Oscar Levant, and Sandy Koufax.

You are not afraid of work, but you rebel at any hint of becoming servile. You are practical in an almost terrifying sense. Which means you can wait, be patient—you can eventually realize your goal despite obstacles, advice, cajoling, pleading. You make up your mind, set your sights, and it is almost impossible to stop you. Some of your key words are ambition, reserve, inward strength, aspiration, attainment, responsibility. These words, though heady and almost symbolic rather than literal, do possess very real meaning for you.

Capricorn is said to govern the joints, the bones, the sense of hearing, the knees, the body system. One of the hazards to your health is rheumatism, an inclination to overindulge where eating and drinking are concerned.

You are sex-conscious in that you regard sex as an important part of your life, part of your happiness, part of your ultimate fulfillment. On the negative side, you tend to think of sex as an end in itself. It is then that you are taken, deceived, made unhappy—given a roller-coaster ride in the sense that you become dizzy, confused.

Sex, you discover when you respond on the positive side, is part of love, a very real part, but not all of it, not something separate or casual but, instead, something warm, a part of life. It involves one part of the horoscope, one section, one department, and is not the entire story, not the entire chart, not the complete wheel of the horoscope.

Listen, Capricorn: I have said you have an affinity with time. This is important because your ruling planet, Saturn, is connected with time, trials, and tribulations. But no matter how many obstacles there are in your way, you'll make a decision, set a goal, and you'll overcome those obstacles. You see, Capricorn: you are an individual who has a feeling of destiny, of purpose. You feel you have a reason for being, an important one. Time becomes your ally. You can be patient and persistent. And this applies, among other things, to the opposite sex. Your Fifth Solar

House—having to do with love, adventure, speculation—
is Taurus. This means the ruling planet of your Fifth House
is Venus. And, in turn, this indicates that your love habits
are strong . . . and necessary . . . as much a part of you
as eating and sleeping and working. Some may not realize it, Capricorn, but you are a sensuous person. You are
capable, to a great extent, of living on love. You can, as a
matter of fact, do without food and sleep to a greater
degree than you can without love. And this provides us
with a clue. You use love as you do food. You often place
the object of your affection *second* to affection itself. You
seem, at times, to be off in a world by yourself. It is not
always easy for people you love to communicate with you,
to feel your presence except in a physical sense. Of course
a highly developed Capricorn is aware of this and makes
amends, corrects this fault, becomes present in more than
a physical or sexual sense.

I have pointed out that Capricorn women, at times, are
accused of being materialistic. But, more often than not,
the charge is false. These women are concerned with the
security of people they love. They are aware of *tomorrow* as
well as today. And, as I say, Capricorn people in general
appear to have a link with the future. Capricorn men
are eager to experience life, not merely to accept someone
else's word about it. That's why the men of this sign are
ambitious enough to struggle in the face of outrageous
odds. They have tremendous faith in themselves, for it is
a faith hammered and shaped through hard knocks, vision,
and a link with destiny.

Now, you may be asked . . . isn't that a bit dramatic?
Well, Capricorn, you do possess a keen sense of drama.

Capricorn

Life is a drama—*your* life is a drama. You can take the blows, the setbacks, because you're sure you're going somewhere. And this is true no matter how much, at times, you may appear to wander in an endless circle. Those are times when you get a second wind, when you take stock, when you pull in your horns and prepare for another assault . . . when you know, yet again, that time is on your side and that, eventually, you will arrive at your goal, your destination. Because, as I say, you do know there is a goal, a place to go, and that you're going to get there. You are, in a sense, vindicated by time. This, of course, is not to imply that you can sit idly by and wait . . . and wait. You must be aware. Aware of the right moment, aware, that there will be a time for action as well as patience. You are blessed in the sense that you know that time heals wounds, that time matures, nourishes, turns the bitter into the sweet.

Listen, Capricorn: you require faith. Otherwise, you drift. You need love. Otherwise you turn to lust. You need an awareness of time. Otherwise, you are aimless. You need responsibility. Otherwise you lose that precious instinct for your personal destiny. Your needs are many and subtle. You are not ordinary in any sense. And often you travel the full circle, returning to the past: to people, triumphs, defeats. The song sings—your ear is attuned. The song leads you to the rocks of despair, or out to the open sea, to freedom.

Listen: the worst is not likely to occur. You can approach the brink but, somehow, there always is a way out. Don't cross bridges before you get to them. Avoid being negative, overcome any tendency to worry and brood. Put a saline solution on your problems—they vanish. But if you start sinking in them—you're sunk.

Family harmony, Capricorn, especially early in life, often is a stranger to you. Yet, you are needed, depended on, even if as a whipping boy. But if the truth be known, you would rather serve than be served. You can be disappointed, poor, a temporary failure. But your time arrives and you are elated, rich, a success. In love, give and receive. Throw off the character armor. Your greatest gift is yourself. When you give of yourself, there is not ridicule, but appreciation. You are controversial, but also appreciated. You are many things to many people, but you are not ignored. And you wouldn't have it any other way.

Analyzing you, Capricorn, can become a breathless task. This is another apparent contradiction. That calm exterior of yours is ripped away and we are confronted with excitement, a kaleidoscope of emotions. No, you are not "easy." You can be tough and soft, giving, and restricted. You are secret, yet open. You are practical, but much concerned with psychological areas. You remember slights, but you balance this by never forgetting a good turn. You can appear morose, but—in a flash—a smile could erase all trace of gloom. You are familiar with trouble but you can handle it in an almost amazing manner. You bounce back with a resiliency that startles. You can get to the top and, when you do, you can hold court with such regality that even a Leo is put to shame. Your personal odyssey is exciting, meaningful, filled with the stuff of life.

THE CAPRICORN LOVER

Here are some secret hints for women about men born under Capricorn: the Capricorn man may start slowly, but you can bet he'll be around at the finish. He is earthy, can possess a keen sense of awareness, is human and warm, and can be depended on to help the underdog and to fight for people he loves. Tact is important in dealing with this man. He may sound brash, he may appear tough, but when it comes to women, be expects them to be tactful, loving, tender, and aware of his particular charms. Once you hook up with this man, you may find yourself hooked for good. He is more sensitive than you might at first suspect. He often laughs at himself, shrugs off sympathy, and gives the impression of being immune to pain. However, he is not only personally sensitive, but transfers this sense of feeling to others: he can look at you, and at others, and somehow discern when things are not right. This produces a dissipating effect: he tends to wear down, to worry more about others than about himself. The first reaction is admiration for this man's apparent nobility. But if you are really interested in his welfare, you should encourage him to face his own problems. Don't let him seek an out. That is, he sometimes busies himself in helping others instead of getting down to the business of his own problems. Make him face himself, make him answer his own questions. An important hint is this: let him talk about himself and help him to help himself. Then you are almost sure of winning him.

Now, let's turn to the other side. This is for men only about women born under Capricorn. This is an earthy woman, not necessarily demonstrative, but she is permanent in the sense that she will not run out on you. She may appear aloof, cold, disinterested, but the fire of passion runs through her veins, and she is a woman in the best sense. Listen, men: look for someone else if you want the frivolous, if you desire someone who can give you a line. This woman, the Capricorn woman, has something special to offer if you are concerned with the future. But she is not for you if you are merely dabbling, experimenting, looking for an interlude. There are many things this woman is, but there is one thing she is not: she is not cold. She is warm, considerate, can rise to the heights of passion. This surprises many because, very often, her exterior is cold. She is earthy in temperament. She is basically independent, original in her thinking, and can break from tradition as quickly as some people drink a cup of coffee. She respects time and tradition in one sense, but believes in creating her own rhythm, her own time, her own tradition. Listen, men: you'd better take a second look at that quiet-appearing Capricorn woman! She may appear cool, but she's smoldering on the inside! There is energy and warmth here—this woman can perceive your character. She can know you and love you and be loyal to you. *But she does expect you to be a man.* She also has a tendency to be curious about the bank account. This is because she is aware of the future, is concerned about tomorrow as well as today.

Your Rising Sign

All persons born under your sign are not exactly the same, although basic characteristics will hold. A horoscope, in actuality, is a map of the sky based on the time and place of birth. If you are aware of your birth time, here are some variations it may cause in your life and character:

Capricorn

Born between 4:00 and 6:00 A.M., your Rising Sign is likely to be the same as your Sun Sign, which is Capricorn, associated with Saturn. This intensifies the characteristics described in this section. You are more idealistic than is the average native of your sign, and more susceptible. That is, you tend to see the best in people, situations. You let down your guard more often; you are hurt, disillusioned to a greater extent than is the average native of this zodiacal sign. Although basically cautious, caution is thrown to the winds when you feel you have found the "right person." Your appearance is apt to be saturnine. But, inside, you bubble with expectation. Real pleasure has been denied you to a great extent. Thus, when you sense pleasure, joy, satisfaction—you go all the way. Hopefully, you have selected the right situation, the right person. But, as you can probably attest, this is not always the case. You are, however, capable of rebounding, of coming back, of reviving, of going on, until, time or your timing coincides with your desires and ambitions and your life can be happy. Know this inwardly and it can be so!

Born between 6:00 and 8:00 A.M., your Ascendant is apt to be Aquarius, associated with the planet Uranus. This combines with your Saturn Solar significator to make you more flexible and active than the average native of your sign. You are daring, restless, inventive—you look for shortcuts but will take any path in order to reach your goal. Although you respect tradition, you refuse to follow it blindly. You love to experiment, to investigate, to strive for the impossible. You are concerned with the occult, and with modern scientific developments. You are, in effect, original in your ideas, willing to try the new against a framework of the tried-and-true. You are progressive, but sentimental. You will help someone from the past, even though you are aware of the fact that the individual has passed the point of being useful. The key is that you are aware. You attract friends with unusual interests, occupations. And you are considered far from the "beaten path" yourself.

Born between 8:00 and 10:00 A.M., your Rising Sign is apt to be Pisces, ruled (measured) by Neptune. This combines with your Saturn significator to make you more perceptive than the average native of your sign. You know what you want for your own comfort and security; you know where and how to obtain it. You also are attached to your family. And you constantly seek approval from the domestic front. You are more philosophical than is the average Capricorn; you blend realism with illusion. You could write; you are intrigued by symbolism and make a fine interpreter of poetry and art. This combination—Neptune and Saturn—is a blend of the practical and the visionary. Naturally, this makes balance a requisite. But balance is delicate and not easy to achieve. It's necessary for you to be able to distinguish between fact and fiction, reality and illusion. You are magnetic, more appealing than many under your sign. You are also more subject to shattered dreams.

Born between 10:00 A.M. and 12:00 noon, your Rising Sign is apt to be Aries, associated with Mars. This combines with your Saturn to make you more aggressive and resourceful than the average native of your sign. You are energetic and determined to achieve goals. You are more original in outlook than is the average member of your zodiacal group. You are apt to be described as militant. In truth, this is because you are active. You are not devoid of a temper. But, on the positive side, this is really inspiration. You become taken up by causes. You can organize activities in a professional manner. Many claim you have a military mind. Again, this could be a misinterpretation of the fact that you can be precise, persistent. You have an insatiable desire for victory. You would rather be right than idealistic. Basically, you can handle responsibility but you expect to be rewarded.

Born between 12:00 noon and 2:00 P.M., your Ascendant or Rising Sign is probably Taurus, associated with Venus. This combines with your Saturn significator to make you more appreciative of art than the average native of your sign. You are also apt to be more sensuous than the average member of your zodiacal sign. You know the value of money and have a knack for obtaining it. You collect; objects of art are included among your "collecting passions." You can be stubborn, you can overindulge and you can go to extremes. As a matter of fact, you seldom do anything in a moderate or lukewarm manner. You live life to the hilt. You take chances. But you constantly keep an eye on future security. Which means that no matter what you do, you are likely to keep that proverbial nest egg. You are earthy: you enjoy eating and loving; you are persistent and obstinate. You are all of those things, but you are also capable of loving and being loved.

Born between 2:00 and 4:00 P.M., your Rising Sign is apt to be Gemini, making you more perceptive than the average native of your sign. Your mind is quicker. Your likes and dislikes are subject to change. You can be conservative, but you tend to believe rules were made for others. You possess wit; you are flexible, more so than the usual person associated with your zodiacal sign. You have a sense of humor, which others describe as "weird." A more apt description, perhaps, is "far out." You are droll. You are a combination of the serious and the hilarious. And the twain does meet. You fear closed spaces; you don't want to be restricted. You are freedom-loving. You can handle responsibility, but you insist on your own style. You revere individuality. You will break tradition, but respect experience. You are shrewd and know how to utilize your unique capabilities.

Born between 4:00 and 6:00 P.M., your Rising Sign is probably Cancer, associated with the Moon. This combines with your Saturn significator to make you more positive, independent, sure than is the average native of your sign. You are possessive; you feel you know what is right. Your affinity with time is heightened. You feel you know how everything will "turn out." You are patient to the point of exasperation. Many are irritated with this attitude. But you are oblivious to criticism along this line. That's the way it is, you seem to be saying. You are conscious of family needs. You want to build a tradition of your own. You are fond of history, of antiques. You feel the basics, such as food and shelter, outweigh the more sensational aspects of life. You are creative; you can successfully appear before and serve the public. You possess qualities of leadership. You would be aided, however, by a more flexible attitude.

Capricorn

Born between 6:00 and 8:00 P.M., your Rising Sign is likely to be Leo, ruled by the Sun. This combines with your Saturn to make you more desirous of public popularity than the average native of your sign. You possess great dignity. But you are less reserved than the typical member of your zodiacal group; many come to you for advice. This gives you a feeling of satisfaction. You are fond of leading, directing, setting policy. You are a natural executive. You fare much better working for yourself than for others. You tend to be fixed in your ways, but possess a natural sense of showmanship. You are more gregarious than is the classic native of your sign. You dispense orders, but the tone is that of a suggestion. You expect your suggestions to be followed. Your capabilities point to success because once you decide on a goal, there is very little veering: you go straight and tolerate few distractions.

Born between 8:00 and 10:00 P.M., your Ascendant is likely to be Virgo, associated with Mercury. This combines with your Saturn significator to make you more creative than is the average native of your sign. You express yourself in a manner that compels attention. You are attractive to the opposite sex. You are a fighter for justice. You are discriminating, aware of personal requirements. This causes some to consider you "fussy." You are dexterous; you express yourself in definite terms. You are steadfast; you are aware of details, of subtle nuances. You are persistent enough to attain goals. But, at times, you outsmart yourself. That is, in seeking perfection, you often lost sight of what is available. Your major objectives are often closer than you imagine. If you can learn to accept and utilize what is here now, you will be happier. Your powers of reasoning are admirable. The key is to act on what you know-without constantly waiting for that proverbial ship to come in; enjoy yourself today!

Born between 10:00 P.M. and 12:00 midnight, your Ascendant or Rising Sign is apt to be Libra, associated with Venus. This combines with your Saturn Solar horoscope rule make you more sociable than the average native of your sign. You seek design, justice, reason; you are analytical. You want reasons; you are not satisfied merely to know that something occurred. You want to know why. Your intellectual curiosity is a mainstay of your character. You are attractive, aware of appearance. Saturn and Venus make an unusual combination: this depicts beauty and discipline and attracts you strongly to law. You are a seeker of justice and you could crusade to correct social ills. You can be practical, but you also have a love of beauty. You are apt to be ultrasensitive. You don't give yourself easily, but once you are committed to a cause or a person, it is all the way. Many people have varying opinions of you: some think of you as stern, withdrawn. Others are positive that you are an unfolding flower, soft and tender. Somewhere, in between, is the real you.

Born between 12:00 midnight and 2:00 A.M., your Rising Sign is apt to be Scorpio, associated with Pluto. This combines with your Saturn significator to make you more volatile than the average native of your sign. You are also versatile, flexible, ambitious, determined to spread, broaden, multiply interests and influences. You will not be contained and you are insistent on having your views mean something. You are idealistic; your ideals are what count. You act on impulse and think later. Your impulses are often beneficial and bring you gain, advantages. You never succeed when blocked, restricted, or afraid. You are capable of earning and attracting money. But you are not as skillful at saving it. However, you make wonderful contacts and get good tips, advice. Again, though, because of your impulsive nature . . . you don't always follow good advice. You are dynamic, attractive to the opposite sex, and not without a temper. Basically, you are sincere and charming. With self-restraint, you could also be successful.

Born between 2:00 and 4:00 A.M., your rising sign is likely to be Sagittarius, associated with Jupiter. This combines with your Saturn significator to make you more discerning than the average native of your sign. You are able to perceive when something of importance is about to occur. You are a natural teacher. You have an insatiable appetite for knowledge and you can inspire others to learn. You benefit through travel, higher education. You could succeed in publishing, public relations, and advertising. You are attracted to politics and feel in tune with world affairs. Your view is universal as opposed to provincial. Your sense of timing is excellent. You seem able to be at the right place at the right time. You could write and entertain; you are not satisfied to be limited. You would discard security for adventure and romance. You are a humanitarian but far from a bleeding heart. You are practical in your efforts to aid the underdog. You are somewhat a dreamer, but capable of making many of your dreams come true.

CAPRICORN FRIENDS AND PARTNERS

Capricorn is harmonious in relation to Scorpio, Pisces, Taurus, and Virgo. Your sign is not well-aspected to Aries, Libra, or Cancer. Capricorn is considered neutral in relation to Sagittarius, Aquarius, Gemini, and Leo.

With another Capricorn, you tend to make wonderful plans, but they could lack solidity. The relationship leaves much to be desired, though it could succeed if each Capricorn is determined to carry through on his or her promises. In actuality, it may be a case of too many leaders and not enough followers. Obviously, this means both want to lead, direct and dominate. A decision must be made as to which one is boss. Once this is done, the relationship could flourish.

CAPRICORN CAREERS

The Tenth House of a horoscope has to do, among other things, with career, ambitions, prestige, standing in the community, and general success through occupational efforts. The Tenth House of your Solar horoscope is Libra, associated with the planet Venus. With Libra on the cusp of your Tenth House, you are more artistic, creative than might be readily apparent. You can change with the times, you keep up with the times, you can measure and judge, and you are attracted to fields associated with government, law, and politics.

Fundamentally, you are practical. You want facts before you predict results. You are capable of responsible leadership; your ideals are high and you don't ask anything of others you are not prepared to do yourself.

You have qualities that make you a natural executive. You are capable of assuming leadership, of handling responsibility. You usually rise from the ranks, often suffering setbacks before achieving major goals. You succeed in politics, as a realtor, builder, contractor, leather goods manufacturer, efficiency expert, grain dealer, watch or clock maker, coal or ice executive, excavator, labor leader, or farmer. Your best work is done at night. You can wait for your cycle to rise, for your ship to come in. You are not easily discouraged; many fine writers, artists, actors, and politicians under your sign have overcome early handicaps to rise to positions of prominence.

Other occupations associated with Capricorn include architect, ceramic engineer, chiropractor, law officer, public health nutritionist, vocational counselor, nuclear safety engineer, and personnel director.

THE CAPRICORN HAND

Some astrologers are proficient at guessing Sun signs; that is, they can look at an individual and perceive his or her zodiacal sign. This is no easy task—it requires experience, practice. The reason is that the Rising Sign (at the time and place of birth) affects personality and appearance, as does the sign the Moon occupied at birth. Yet, the place of the Sun is a strong indicator where character and appearance enter the picture.

Over the years, I have found that one significant key in this effort is the human hand. A person's hand often reveals whether that individual was born under a Fire, Earth, Air, or Water Sign.

You, Capricorn, were born under an Earth Sign; Capricorn belongs to the Earth element. The Earth-type hand is generally large, square, practical.

The Earth Trinity is comprised of Capricorn, Virgo, and Taurus. The hand is square-shaped; the hands are wide rather than long. The thumb is not flexible. (A square jaw is also an identifying mark of your sign.) The thumb does not bend back. It depicts a certain amount of obstinacy. The Capricorn hand has a large mount of Venus, which is the largest blood vessel in the hand, located beneath the thumb. The mount under the second finger (mount of Saturn) is also usually well developed.

This is a hand which looks like it "means business." That's Capricorn and that is the Capricorn hand.

CAPRICORN SECRETS

The horoscope, with its twelve angles or Houses, covers every area of life, including your secrets. The Twelfth House holds sway over secret fears fantasies, problems, all that is hidden or beneath the surface.

In your case, Sagittarius occupies the Twelfth House; the Jupiter of Sagittarius combines with your Saturn significator to show that one of your secrets is a belief that you know how everything is due to turn out—that, indeed, you know the end before the middle before the beginning; that you can see ahead and perceive results and that you go along with ordinary mortals out of a kind of courtesy, as a convenience, so as not to startle, but that you do know what the outcome is to be. This prescience (real or imagined) is one of your basic secrets.

A secret desire is to travel, to learn, to gain secret information, to write, read, publish; you, in your fantasies, are the crusader who rights the ills of the world through communication and education. You are, in your Walter Mitty life, an educator, a writer, a foreign correspondent, a Robin Hood, ever willing to give to the poor and deprive the rich.

One of your secrets is to interpret, to dramatize, to symbolize your time, and to influence it. You want to be expansive, almost the opposite of the appearance you give, that of restricting, disciplining. You want, in your inner or secret self, to stretch the rules. By all outward appearances, you are conservative, willing to follow the rules. Inwardly, you are expansive, more than willing to skip or break the rules, intent on humanitarian acts, determined to fulfill charitable motives. You are, if your secrets be known, a teacher, a sage, perhaps a prophet.

One of your fears is that you will not be able to communicate your great and grand intentions. This causes you to bottle up your emotions, to tighten and tense. The remedy is to do your best, sincerely and well, to be pleased with yourself and not to care too much about the impression made on others.

Your major secret, your fantasy, is seeing yourself bubbling with laughter, handing out gifts, traveling the length and breadth of the land with messages of peace and goodwill. Your *fear* is that you are not giving enough, that you are not living up to your self-image.

Your secrets are those which have to do with life. You are so inwardly expansive that you suffer embarrassment when this secret, sacred side of yourself is threatened with exposure. You want to rise above petty obstacles; you want to soar (and you so picture yourself), to be able to give and to provide happiness. Your secrets involve life and humanity. To those who lack sensitivity, you appear to be (at times) hard, self-contained, morose. To those who do possess sensitivity, you are seen as warm, giving, reticent, shy, reluctant to expose yourself for fear of being misunderstood.

Your secret really is that you would like to give completely and not fear being taken advantage of, not fear ridicule, not fear embarrassment. Your secrets are on a grand scale—nothing petty. Your desire is not for power, but for goodwill. You want to teach, to spread knowledge, to make the world a better place in which to live.

It becomes clear that your secrets involve your being an idealist, a humanist, one who would transcend the rules, the red tape, in order to perform deeds that are uplifting. You keep those secrets very well because many regard you as cool, calculating. You are, of course, the opposite. But do recognize your secrets; you needn't be so intent on suppressing them. Let go; they are wonderful secrets and should not be transformed into fears.

Aquarius
January 20 - February 18

Birthstone
Amethyst

Flower
Violet

Numbers
1, 2, and 7

Color
Electric Blue

Parts of Body
Legs and Calves

Cities
Bremen, Hamburg,
Brighton, Buenos Aires,
Georgetown

Countries
Russia, Sweden, Abyssinia

Your Character and Life

You were born under a sign often associated with astrology and astrologers. Aquarius is the natural eleventh zodiacal sign, associated with the planet Uranus. It is electric and its natives can be shocking because they are likely to be unorthodox. While a Capricorn is associated with time, in the sense of having patience, the ability to play a waiting game, an Aquarian can be sudden, like a bolt from the blue, revealing a dynamic that creates attention through the unexpected.

It is not easy for astrologers to pinpoint Aquarius: there is something of the astrologer in members of this sign and there is something of Aquarius in most astrologers. The most famous American astrologer was the late Evangeline Adams, who was an Aquarian. Gertrude Stein was another Aquarian. She made much of the world aware of what could be done with the English language. Aquarius is associated with aviation as well as astrology; Charles Lindberg was an Aquarian. Aquarius natives are involved with electricity and television; the sign stands for progress. The Uranian influence—in the sense that Aquarius reaches out into the future—is one of progress, tomorrow rather than today. Aquarius stands for social justice, the future—in the way that the future is envisioned by inventors (Thomas Edison was an Aquarian), poets, writers, artists, social critics. You are contemporary, to say the least: Jack Lemmon, Carol Channing, and Victor Mature are but a few "modern" celebrities born under your sign. More people (and celebrities) are born during the period from January 20–February 18 than during any other time of the year.

Aquarius

Aquarius is the natural, eleventh zodiacal sign, associated with friends, hopes, wishes, aspirations. Your sign, thus, has an electric quality, contains an element of surprise, is fixed and is of the Air element. You can be stubborn, fixed in your views; but you are also able to listen to reason, to perceive the future, to be sensitive to the needs of others.

You attract and repel persons for the same reasons. You are anything but orthodox. You are eccentric in the sense that, though surrounded by people, you refuse to "follow the crowd." You are attractive to the opposite sex, but you can also be friends with them. You arouse jealousy. You need praise, appreciation. You want friends but you will not conform. You are progressive, but you will not knowingly destroy. You are intuitive, but you don't claim to be psychic.

You are difficult to "pin down" because, very often, you do not know what you are going to do next. You are associated with action, although you can be fixed in your ways. Your forte is the surprise. You have a sense of comedy, you catch people "off guard."

You are like the color associated with your sign, *electric blue*. There is an air of excitement about you . . . also the challenge, possibly the danger one can sense around electricity. You are electric—you're concerned with aviation, television, progress, space: you are somewhat occult, a scientist, practical and fantastic. Your metal is uranium and you are as unique as that metal. You are generous (but usually have an eye on, say, dividend possibilities). You take a chance, but in the sense that a pioneer is willing to experiment, to give birth to an invention.

Kim Novak was born under your sign, exemplifying a vital, inventive, artistic rebelliousness, in the sense of deciding for one's self rather than adhering to the rules. Aquarian astrologer Evangline Adams said of you that Aquarians should never take the advice of others against their own intuition or judgment. Some of the greatest mistakes, she asserted, are likely to come through being misguided because of lack of confidence. You, Aquarius, must have confidence in your own spiritual and mental powers. It is when you go against your own inner feelings that you invite difficulty. Aquarius is associated with the calves of the leg in particular, but also is connected with the vessels of the body that carry fluid of any kind—especially the lymphatic system.

You possess a unique ability: the ability to convince. You often work with institutions, organizations rather than individuals. You admire large organizations, but prefer to be treated yourself as an individual. At times you are so concerned with the picture as a whole that you neglect details.

You prefer to warm up during real action. Rehearsals tend to leave you cold. You want the real thing. You want the situation, the experience to be white-hot. You crackle, shine, you are bright with promise, but dark with secrets others have confided. You are a friend and lover, a protector and romanticist. You are one of the most fascinating of the members of the zodiacal signs; and as a person, despite your amiable front, you are difficult to analyze, to classify—your breadth of vision is so wide that, to many observers, the picture becomes incomprehensible.

You want to give pleasure but expect your reward for so doing. You can be fanciful or, on the negative side, a deceiver. Your motives, Aquarius, are good, but the road to good intentions is often paved with the broken glass of shattered promises.

Aquarius

Listen, Aquarius: once you possess your heart's desire, you tend to look to greener fields. Once the challenge is gone, once the game is over, you tend to seek a now contest, a new challenge, a new game.

You could, if not careful, have a *Don Juan* complex. You are not conventional. You are often not capable of secret intrigue because you are an idealist—what you do, you want to be out in the open. This, in a conventional society, could pose problems. Listen, Aquarius: you are sophisticated, yet you retain enough childlike wonder to be fascinated by the new, the unusual, the strange, the enchanting. You are a seeker of knowledge, but usually in unorthodox ways.

Your tendency is to be subjective rather than objective. You experience flashes of knowledge. Your intuition is strong, but you don't always act on it. By this, Aquarius, I am telling you that you often act in a manner at cross purposes to your own best interests. Heed your own inner voice. The best advice you receive comes, from within. Others sometimes can't keep up with you. Your Uranian nature places you at the head of the crowd. While others are contemplating a move, you are making it. While others wonder, you discover. This being so, it is not wise for you to expect everyone to understand, to comprehend, to judge accurately your feelings and motives. The judge of you, Aquarius, must be you.

You want to be courageous, attractive, high-principled. But what you want, and the manner in which you act, are not always the same. You must not be afraid of failure. Let that sink in, Aquarius. With adventure, the fear of failure must be erased from your mind. Constant fear in this direction adds up to false pride. Take a chance. Take steps. Invest in your own abilities. Assert yourself. Then, win or lose, you are ultimately the victor. Otherwise, it is a matter of win or lose—and you are still the loser. Listen, Aquarius: where you are concerned, a grand failure is better than a petty success. Try reach out. Utilize your vision. Encompass greater goals.

There is a crackling excitement about Aquarians. Not everyone can take them, but very few can completely leave them alone. Aquarians tend to excite our dreams, to bring color to our visions, to make real our fantasies. So, you see, Aquarius, you're quite an individual. The planet that is associated with your sign, Uranus, is the planet representing surprise, sudden action, a breaking away from the mold, a peek into the future.

Now, like all of you, you do possess your faults, weaknesses. One of these is your insatiable desire to make people aware of you. Carried to extremes . . . this causes you to blow up your own importance, perhaps in the wrong areas. For example, you may pose as an expert. You might cry crocodile tears. You can, on the negative side, do things for *effect* rather than for a purpose You will battle in flurries rather than sustaining your attack. You will change sides, you will change your mind—you will be confused, then, rather than inventive and versatile.

The key, Aquarius, is to give others time to know you, to grow with you. Then you won't have to battle to impress, won't have to go out of your way to do so. Once you learn this lesson—the lesson of being true to yourself and letting others know the real you instead of a counterfeit version—then you will have learned a most valuable truth. Once this lesson is learned, you'll learn to overcome envy. You'll learn to be true to yourself, sincere, a visionary instead of an opportunist.

You see, Aquarius, you want to pounce on opportunity. You want to be where the action is. And this is all to the good. But when you fail to define your terms, to outline your goals, then you tend to be eccentric rather than brilliant, scattered rather than centered, a mere dilettante rather than one who is masterful and knowledgeable. When you find yourself rushing about in circles, ask yourself *why.* Slow down. Get to the heart of your motives. Those who continue to fail to understand you are not the people you need in the first place. So why knock yourself out trying to get them to understand? Those who are right for you will perceive your meaning, will encourage and warm you . . . will have faith. When this occurs, Aquarius, the mad rush will cease, the ring-around-the-rosy will be relegated to its proper child's place, and you will emerge a mature individual.

You like to gamble, but want the rules made your way. You don't mind losing, but you do not want to suffer in loss. You accept conventions, but for other people. You respect laws, but don't want to be restrained by them. You learn rules, but want to break them. You want money, but don't want to undergo the inconvenience of saving it. You dislike ostentation in others, but you yourself want to be seen or heard, no matter what the cost. You must learn to trust others rather than to scheme about them. Your potential is so great that it is a crime to anchor yourself down to petty desires, petty faults, petty motives. You can and should be one of the grand ladies or men of your time.

You can be demanding where friends are concerned, yet take it for granted that they will overlook your shortcomings. You are original, independent, desirous of progress. But, you'll become only a shell of your real potential. Astrologers are fond of your sign because Aquarius is related to astrology itself. Many born under Aquarius, as we have stated, are famous individuals, and many of these are fascinated with astrology. Kim Novak is but one example. Actress Susan Oliver is another; in fact, her mother, Ruth Hale Oliver, was a fine astrologer. The list could be extended: it includes some of the brightest names, some of the most fascinating people of our time.

Aquarius—you are remarkable, but not everyone has the strength to see you through. You enjoy the spotlight, but have been known to complain that it hurts your eyes. You are a mass of psychological ups and downs, contradictions and affirmations. You possess an ingratiating manner, win friends, and influence people. But you must be prepared to accept the responsibility for such victories. Otherwise, you are going to be lonely; you will win in a superficial manner, while what you require is depth and sincerity.

If you want to start really to fulfill your potential. I would advise this kind of beginning: learn to crawl and then to walk. Learn lessons thoroughly. Get up and walk; then you can run, taking happiness and prosperity by the hand as your boon companions. You can finally fulfill yourself, Aquarius, if only you'll take time to learn the rules before breaking them. If you do this, you will fly high and soar over any obstacles. You are the individual who defies the odds, who creates the upset. You are unpredictable because you have something in reserve. You don't always show your best side, but it is there—and you can surprise us by displaying it when least expected.

THE AQUARIUS LOVER

I advise men about Aquarius women to be charming, imaginative in their entertainment plans. Remember, men: the Aquarius woman lives in a world where dreams can—and often do—come true. If you are drab in manner, in entertaining, in presenting your ideas and ambitions . . . she is likely to think you a fool. Or worse, a bore. Knowing the Aquarius woman could change your life. She is a stimulant in the manner that cold, bubbly wine is—and, men, before you know it she'll go to your head! Listen: the Aquarian woman likes to have her own way. When she is right, let her have her way. But, when you feel she is wrong, fight her every inch of the way. The Aquarian woman enjoys a good fight. It has a tonic effect on her and she'll look at you—and up to you—with new respect. She'll lead you in circles if she can get away with it. Tell her where you stand, what it is you want and expect, and you'll be on the way to a happy, fruitful relationship.

Those were special hints for men about Aquarian women. Now, let's reverse the procedure. Here are hints for woman about the Aquarian male: the Aquarius man has the ability to know without benefit of formal study. His knowledge is subjective; it comes from within. His special credits and his abilities are not academic. The Aquarius man learns by doing, feeling, experimenting, making as many mistakes as any beginner, yet displaying a master's feel for a subject. He is concerned with hopes, wishes, friends, loyalty, and promises. A broken promise can mean a broken friendship as far as the Aquarian man is concerned. Don't say one thing to him and do another. No matter how innocent, no matter how noble your intentions are, the Aquarius man can interpret your word to the letter. If that word is broken, it is a serious affair with him.

He isn't easy to get along with. He can be a bully; he can be absent-minded. Sometimes his mind is so much on the future that he tends to overlook the present completely. Be sure he doesn't forget you. Let him be aware of your presence. Make sure he doesn't bypass you. Make yourself a part of his plans, for he is constantly planning, dreaming, inventing, devising, prophesying. Listen: don't expect the Aquarius man to be perfect. He has his faults and these can be exasperating. However, he is generous, reasonable, willing to help, to listen to your problems, to become involved, to offer advice. You'll have to teach him to be practical. If left to his own devices, he might give everything away. He makes friends with those others are apt to consider mere cranks. He can work and fight against odds—but he requires someone to have faith in him. And that is where you come in if you are serious about the Aquarian man.

Your Rising Sign

All persons born under your sign are not exactly the same, although basic characteristics will hold. A horoscope, in actuality, is a map of the sky based on the time and place of birth. If you are aware of your birth time, here are some variations it may cause in your life and character:

Born between 4:00 and 6:00 A.M., your Rising Sign is apt to be Aquarius, the same as your Sun Sign, associated with Uranus. This intensifies the characteristics described in this section. You are always willing to break with tradition. You can tear down in order to rebuild. You are more daring than the usual native of your sign. You also are impulsive, filled with a kind of magnetism that attracts the opposite sex. You make surprise moves, you are inventive. You look beyond the immediate and perceive future trends. You will go to extremes when you feel the cause is right. You possess a rare quality; when convinced you are wrong, you will admit it and change tactics. This can be a great key to ultimate success. You are not committed to one course; you follow a path only when you feel it is progressive, constructive. You are idealistic, but you are also practical. You prefer to transform dreams into realities rather than merely to dream. That's part of your inventive quality and it can propel you to the limelight of recognition.

Born between 6:00 and 8:00 A.M., your Ascendant or Rising Sign is apt to be Pisces, giving Neptune as your significator. This combines with your Uranus Solar ruler to make you more sensitive to the needs of others than is the average native of your sign. You have a universal appeal. You attract people to you with their problems. You often carry more than your fair share of burdens. You are intuitive and may claim you possess extrasensory perception. Your disposition is definitely along humanitarian lines. You are more interested in feeding the hungry than in reforming them. You can be secretive. You don't expose your true nature to everyone. Many different people see you in different lights. You are, to say the least, somewhat a mystery. And this could also apply to yourself: you don't always recognize your own motives, aspirations. You find expression through unorthodox lines. But you do express!

Born between 8:00 and 10:00 A.M., your Rising Sign is apt to be Aries, ruled by Mars. This combines with your Uranus significator to make you more dynamic than the average native of your sign. That is, you act in a more direct, forceful manner. You also tend to be aggressive. You state your point and follow through. But you also have a quality of receptiveness which many lack. You are willing to listen as well as to assert. You are zealous and somewhat a reformer. You have the ability to sway and convince. You can make a gesture, such as raising an eyebrow while listening, which can speak more eloquently than words. You are impatient. You want action. You often act first and think later. You draw to you the undecided. But they don't always remain so very long! You never hesitate in expressing views. And you are proficient at piecing together bits of information and synthesizing them into a complete story. You can detect the needs of others and fulfill them. Many think they can put something over on you—but they learn differently.

Born between 10:00 A.M. and 12:00 noon, your Rising Sign is likely to be Taurus, associated with Venus. This combines with your Uranus Solar significator to make you more determined—and stubborn—than is the average native of your sign. An emphasis here is on your ability to collect, to save, to discover genuine bargains in out-of-the-way places. You are very much aware of money. You are willing to accept pressure, responsibility. Once your mind is made up, nothing seems to deter you. In this sense, you could be said to have a "one-track mind." You are more sensuous than the classic native of your sign. You love luxury, the "good" things of life. You are willing to work for what you get and, where money is concerned, you are all business. Your no-nonsense attitude alienates some, but inspires confidence in those who want their assets protected. You are a natural executive because you have the courage to set policy, and demand that it be followed. You have a knack of finding the right person for a particular job, for maintaining good terms with those who have money to invest in worthwhile projects.

Born between 12:00 noon and 2:00 P.M., your Ascendant is apt to be Gemini, ruled by Mercury. This combines with your Venus significator to give you more of an intellectual bent than the average native of your sign. You are restless, dynamic, and daring. You are willing to test ideas, theories. You also are willing to invest in your own talents. You are a natural teacher, fond of travel, and ready to leave the status quo in exchange for a meaningful challenge. You are more easily able to express yourself than is the average native of your sign. You are not stopped by details; you find ways, means of getting through red tape. You are confident that your view of the future is an accurate one. This is probably because your intuition has come through for you in the past—you have confidence in your intuitive abilities. You are generally optimistic, active, versatile. Imparting knowledge provides you with psychological income—of the more solid variety, too. You are perceptive enough to be practical when it counts.

Born between 2:00 and 4:00 P.M., your Rising Sign is apt to be Cancer, associated with the Moon. This combines with your Uranus indicator to make you more aware of domestic responsibilities than is the average native of your sign. You are capable of plowing through details and coming up with a central theme. You have an ability to appeal to women if you're a man, to harmonize with and to serve them. You can be possessive; you are loyal to your family. You revere tradition, but wish to create your own. This combination brings you publicity, recognition, but creates a desire to try too much at once. You can be patient, but only to a point. Then you break loose and much of what you built in the past could go by the way-side. Your personality or "outer appearance" belies your inner feelings. You give the impression of being stable to the degree of appearing to have little imagination. In actuality, you see the future with ambitions, dreams, aspirations. This, of course, means a conflict. The key is to achieve balance. Be imaginative without losing your practical touch. You can detect it when something is going to grow in value (particularly real estate). Follow through on your hunches. Invest in what you feel will multiply in value.

Born between 4:00 and 6:00 P.M., your Rising Sign is likely to be Leo, associated with the Sun. This combines with your Uranus significator to make you versatile and give you more of a sense of drama than is possessed by the average native of your sign. You are versatile, artistic; you are a natural showman and an excellent salesman. You sell ideas. You sell dreams. You are theatrical and can impress and move large numbers of people. You see projects as a whole, but details tend to leave you cold. You can outline and plan, but the practical, everyday aspects are better off in other hands. Your sense of humor is delightful. You have charm to spare. You are attractive to the opposite sex, and being eccentric is a definite part of your makeup.

You do not follow tradition. You are inventive, optimistic, and one of your best qualities is a zest for living. You are expansive and generous. You are the opposite of petty. You do tend to scatter your forces but, no matter what the situation, you usually land on your feet.

Born between 6:00 and 8:00 P.M., your Rising Sign is apt to be Virgo, related to Mercury. This combines with your Uranus Solar significator to make you more analytical than the average native of your sign. You can be surprisingly introspective. You seek perfection. You are concerned with reasons; you are slow to decide but quick to act once you arrive at a conclusion. You can be so much aware of health that some claim you are bothersome about it. The truth of the matter is that you want security and want to be healthy enough to enjoy it. You are conscious of social justice—or the lack of it. You are a seeker of perfection. You want the books to balance, the relationships to be harmonious. When anything goes out of kilter you become rebellious. You are not easy to deceive, but you are quite capable of fooling yourself. You see people, situations in an idealistic light. You are intrigued by the occult, attracted to history, religion, and law. The theater fascinates you; some of your closest friends could be connected with motion pictures or television. You can be a dynamo. It certainly is not easy to keep up with the pace you set.

Born between 8:00 and 10:00 P.M., your Ascendant is apt to be Libra, associated with the planet Venus. This combines with your Uranus significator to make you determined, responsible, and more intellectually aware than the average native of your sign. You are romantic, but you must respect the object of your affection before love materializes. You have a keen sense of responsibility. You are intense where the opposite sex is concerned. There is little that's halfway in that area; it is all the way or nothing with you. You are a lover of justice. You are attracted to law and you will fight for the underdog. You measure, you time—you size up and you invent ways to bring about equality. This doesn't make you popular in all circles, but you usually are willing to pay for these consequences. You are a born romantic. For you, life is romance, and you have that effect on most others, too. It is hard for others to be around you without feeling your intensity, without responding. You are full of life, and you make others feel alive.

Born between 10:00 P.M. and 12:00 midnight, your Rising Sign is apt to be Scorpio, associated with Pluto. This combines with your Uranus Solar ruler to make you desirous of affection, home, a sense of belonging—more so than the average native of your sign. Your emotions run the gamut, from war to peace. You have a strong creative urge. You find it necessary to express yourself, for good or otherwise. Your acts are not of the routine variety; you are sudden and dramatic. You are creative and inventive. But you have a tendency to discard the useful along with the useless. Obviously, you should learn to be more discriminating. Your artistic appreciation is strong; your love of design is evident. You desire love and a home and family. But you desire these things on your own terms. You can be so stubborn that what you want most . . . you can reject. This is a psychological kink that can be rectified. It'll take some effort on your part, but it can be done. You are attractive, dynamic, magnetic. You become involved in unusual situations and with "strange" people sometimes. You need family backing for genuine satisfaction. Know this and act accordingly.

Born between 12:00 midnight and 2:00 A.M., your Rising Sign is apt to be Sagittarius, associated with Jupiter. This combines with your Uranus significator to make you more perceptive and curious than the average native of your sign. You are especially fond of travel. You communicate. You write, take pictures, perhaps, and analyze. You explain. You want to know the why of things. You are open, direct, frank. Your personal magnetism attracts the opposite sex. You can exude charm, and you have an insatiable appetite for knowledge. You fight any tendency toward lethargy. You would make a fine actor, if you gave that pursuit the necessary time and energy. Politics also intrigues you. You are a natural orator. You compel attention. You would never be satisfied in a routine job. You are an individual to your fingertips. You express that individuality. Others gain inner joy when with you—when you are at your best. Change, travel, and variety are a trio that is a part of you. You write, could photograph well, teach, learn, and communicate. Your sense of drama propels you into the limelight.

Born between 2:00 and 4:00 A.M., your Rising Sign is apt to be Capricorn, ruled by Saturn. This combines with your Uranus significator to make you more direct, determined, and original than the average native of your sign. You set your goal and find unique ways of attaining it. You are aware of time; you use it. Your direction is straight. It is difficult, if not impossible, to deter you. Your ideals are high; you are a natural leader, though your thoughts and methods are anything but orthodox. You are independent in thought and action, and your approach is original. Many consider you too sharply focused on yourself. The truth is that you are willing to make sacrifices to achieve what you want, while others would not think of making those same sacrifices. You can give the impression of being selfish. In fact, you are selfless. You will forego apparent necessities to arrive at a destination. You travel light, but where love is concerned you will stop in your tracks as if you were carrying the heaviest weight. You are not easy to comprehend: fast and slow, sudden and deliberate. It takes time to know you well—only time enables you to find your own voice truly.

AQUARIUS FRIENDS AND PARTNERS

An Aquarius, in a relationship with another born under the same sign, can be highly successful . . . if a third person handles the details. With another Aquarius, you tear down and rebuild. You become master builders. You see beyond the immediate. But you tend to overlook essentials. That's why a third person, proficient in handling details, can be an invaluable aid to two Aquarians embarked on a project. In a personal relationship, there are problems because each Aquarian is so much of an individual—each wants his (or her) own way. Unless there is excitement, adventure the relationship could wither.

Aquarius is favorably aspected to Sagittarius, Aries, Gemini, and Libra. Your sign is not favorably aspected to Taurus, Scorpio, or Leo. Aquarius is neutral in relation to Capricorn, Pisces, Cancer, and Virgo.

Aquarius Careers

The Tenth House of a horoscope has to do, among other things, with career, ambitions, prestige, standing in the community and general success through occupational efforts. The Tenth Sector of your Solar horoscope is Scorpio, associated with the planet Pluto. With Scorpio on the cusp of your Tenth House, you have drive, can be secretive and magnetic, and can appeal to the love of mystery which all of us possess.

Where your career is concerned, you can be a designer of the future, an individual who modernizes. You are modern, you are in advance, in the forefront, the *avant garde*.

Careers associated with Aquarius natives include those of scientist, inventor, astrologer, astronomer, pilot, engineer, lecturer, research worker, nerve specialist, electrical expert, and motion picture producer. You could also find success in television.

You probe secrets. You are fascinated with occupations that require a degree of detective work. You can bring comfort to people's homes: this could include social work as well as interior decorating. You have a natural sense of drama; you can turn the ordinary into the extraordinary—you could be involved in the space program. Other occupations suitable to your sign include astrobiologist, electroplater, nuclear physicist, and air-conditioning technician.

Whatever you do, you do with gusto; there is a kind of passionate belief in your work. You are an asset to your occupation. Don't stay in anything that fails to provide a healthy challenge.

THE AQUARIUS HAND

Some astrologers are proficient at guessing Sun signs; that is, they can look at an individual and perceive his, or her, zodiacal sign. This is no easy task—it requires experience, practice. The reason is that the Rising Sign (at the time and place of birth) affects personality and appearance, as does the sign the Moon occupied at birth. Yet, the place of the Sun is a strong indicator where character and appearance enter the picture.

Over the years, I have found that one significant key in this effort is the human hand. A person's hand often reveals whether that individual was born under a Fire, Earth, Air, or Water Sign.

You, Aquarius, were born under an Air Sign; Aquarius belongs to the Air element. The Air-type hand is the opposite of the Earth element: the Air-element hand is long slender, even delicate; very sensitive, compared with the square, rough, practical hand which belongs to that of the Earth element. The Air or Aquarius hand is triangular; the second finger is longer than the first and much longer than the index or little finger, and the thumb is apt to be flexible.

The Air Trinity (Aquarius, Libra, Gemini) hand has a narrow palm and long fingers. The hand is usually long and thin, with more lines found on the palm than can be found on the hands of the Earth, Water, or Fire Sign hands.

The Aquarius hand can be the hand of an artist, a designer. It is a graceful hand, but it is also purposeful.

AQUARIUS SECRETS

The horoscope, with its twelve angles or Houses, covers every area of life, including your secrets. The Twelfth House holds sway over secret fears, fantasies, undercover problems, all that is hidden or beneath the surface.

In your case, Capricorn occupies the Twelfth House; the Saturn of Capricorn combines with your Uranus significator to show that one of your fears is that your originality and independence will not be put to proper use. You are progressive, but you fear that you will have to face the music of your innovations. With Capricorn signifying your secrets, there is a saturnine "drag." That means that, while you want to make your own traditions, you fear most that which you ridicule. You fear injury to the lower part of your body, your legs. You fear that your legs may not be straight or beautiful . . . you fear poverty. You fear that you spend too freely: and the more you fear in this area, the more extravagant you tend to become. You fear that one of your major secrets will be revealed: it is a secret, or fear, having to do with time. You fear growing old without tasting fully of life.

One of your secrets is your passion. You are, to the observer, an intellectual. Inwardly, you are determined, even morose, passionate in your desire to accomplish goals. One of your secrets is that you feel your theories, desires, ambitions, visions will not be fulfilled for a considerable time. You give the appearance of feeling that your ship is "just over the horizon." But, in reality, you are like the rest of us. You simply cannot see beyond that horizon.

Your secret, basically, is one that has to do with deep, inner feelings. You fear more than you reveal. You can put on an act of indifference, even jubilance, while doubting, haranguing yourself, doubting yourself, and wondering if, indeed, your ideas are correct.

In your fantasies, you are the leader, heading your community, even your nation, being a power with which to contend throughout the world. Listen: you want to run things; that's one of your secrets. You regard secret, and sacred, your feelings that you do, after all is said and done, know what is best. What is good for Aquarius is good for all: that's your secret motto. You want to be first; that's a secret, while Aries (for example) makes no secret of that desire. You appear as an intellectual (which very often you are), but you are willing to bull your way through—you want to base your knowledge on facts, but one of your secrets is that often you act on hearsay.

You fear that you may be taking on more than you can handle. That is a well-kept secret because, on the surface, you give the appearance of being able to fly to the Moon without too much exertion. Another secret is that you are in need, not only of recognition, but of old-fashioned affection. You are modern, that is true. But, secretly, you yearn for discipline. You long for the discipline of tradition. You are pulled in two directions: one is toward freedom, independence. The other is toward responsibility, restriction, safety, a sure way, a way which was proved sufficient in the past: "that old-time religion."

You have many secrets; most are well-kept. You don't reveal too much of your inner feelings. But they are important and perhaps reading this section about yourself will help relieve some of those "quiet burdens." You needn't fear these things.

Pisces

February 19 – March 20

Birthstone
Aquamarine

Flower
Jonquil

Numbers
2, 6, and 7

Color
Sea Green

Parts of Body
Feet

Cities
Alexandria, Worms, Seville,
Lancaster, Regensburg,
Dublin, Birmingham,
Casablanca, Lisbon, Cardiff,
Omaha, Miami

Countries
Portugal, Sahara Desert,
Scotland, Spain, England

YOUR CHARACTER AND LIFE

Some might claim that you tend to drift on occasion, that you may dream more than you act; at times, this is true. But I have found that Pisces people often make their dreams turn to realities, that they are indeed capable of acting out their dreams. What is a dream to many of us is a prophetic vision to a Piscean.

Realize this about yourself. Value your dreams. Take note of them; make them a subject of study and analysis. You are a natural romantic, not in the sense that Leo is. Your romance is of the shimmering, imaginative variety, as contrasted to the direct feel, touch, and display of Leo. Leo is associated with Fire and you with Water; the difference is obvious. Both are necessary, but in different ways.

Many astrologers refer to your sign as that of a mild person. I do not wholly agree. There is nothing lacking in you. You have to be strong to make dreams become realities—and you'll do this a surprising number of times. You have to be strong to sympathize with us when we blunder, when we stubbornly refuse (or seem unable) to perceive your subtle meanings. Yes, you are strong enough—in many, many ways.

You are not just mild. You are understanding, receptive, and you possess more than an ordinary amount of extrasensory perception. You are prescient. You sense it when something of importance is about to occur. You are a detector of trends; you have an instinctive understanding of cycles. The aura of mystery which often surrounds you is something that comes naturally to you. It is not "applied," in the sense that one might apply makeup. It is there, an integral part of you. It is magnetic and draws us to you.

You were born under the twelfth sign of the zodiac, a sign associated with the planet Neptune and, belonging to the Water element. Pisces is fascinating . . . many regard Pisces people as overly sympathetic, easily taken advantage of by unscrupulous people. But I have a different view of you, Pisces. I feel that you are reserved. I feel that your apparent mild manner is really a matter of holding back, of thinking deeply, of analyzing, of playing a key role, sometimes behind the scenes. The Twelfth House is associated with behind-the-scenes activity, with illusion, beauty, sensitivity—with secrets, with a tendency to appear to be quiet while making plenty of noise inside. By this, Pisces, I mean that you don't often exhibit your true strength, or the turmoil that can sometimes rage within.

I have noted that Pisces women often have unusual eyes—something about these women calls attention to their eyes. And while the typical Pisces woman could appear to be quiet, gentle, delicate . . . her eyes are inviting, telling a story of hidden sensuousness, giving a promise of love and passion.

Anais Nin, the writer, was a Piscean and her life, her eyes, her diary, are illustrative of the depth, the capacity to imagine, the romance of Pisces. Miss Nin well knew her own sign, and its planetary symbol, Neptune. She was Piscean, Neptunian—and beautiful. Elizabeth Taylor is another famous Piscean. The Water element shows up here in that she is receptive enough to portray various roles, to receive impressions and to interpret them for us through her Academy Award-winning acting ability.

Jennifer Jones is another example of Pisces. This sign, as we said, is the twelfth sign, and thus in the natural Twelfth House—that section of the chart related, among other things, to the theater, to motion pictures, to illusion, beauty, subtle meaning, and much sensitivity.

Zero Mostel is an example of a male Piscean—an actor who was able to bubble over with impressions and, though large physically, was able to transmit subtle images, delicate nuances, fine-line character portraits. Harry Belafonte, Pamela Mason, and Jackie Gleason are other examples of famous individuals born under your sign.

You have a feeling, Pisces, that others expect you to know more than you do. You are confident, within the confines of your knowledge. But there is that gnawing kind of apprehension that others do expect more, perhaps deserve more than you are capable of giving or explaining. Now, there is a way of interpreting this quality. The astrological textbooks state that you are sympathetic, willing to give up quickly in the case of an argument . . . that you are sometimes shy. But I say that you merely don't want to become involved with people who cannot appreciate your special talents, your unique knowledge, your qualities of sensitivity, and awareness of what is rare.

And, listen, Pisces: you are sensitive enough to know that what I am saying about you is true—so true, so unique that I would wager you even now are smiling the smile of self-recognition.

On the negative side, you are on occasion somewhat limited. On the positive side, you are special. You don't care about the mob, the crowd, about what most people think. You are selective and you appeal to a select group.

You are favored and feared. You could deceive, and be deceived. You love beauty but can become involved in ugly scenes. You are modest, but expansive. You are delicate but strong, fragile but sturdy, vulnerable but robust. You can analyze Pound's poetry in one breath, and complain about your aching feet in the next. (Pisces does rule the feet . . . and many born under your sign do complain, sometimes in a most comical manner, about the fact that their feet hurt.)

Your comments, your attitudes crackle with the dry, white heat of conviction. But you do so with a smile. You are gentle. To some, you appear above reproach. To others, the opposite may be true. You are, on occasion, behind-the-scenes in the sense that you don't reveal yourself— sometimes not even to yourself.

Neptune is your planetary indicator. It is elusive, fragile, but it is there, moving slowly, creating impressions as well as illusions. You are an imaginative person, a magician— you are a poet and writer, a critic, and propagandist. You are capable of being more than one person and, at times, you appeal to heaven above to reveal the true you to you.

You cherish secrets but yearn to be understood, to be revealed and purified. You are patient, capable of waiting, having faith, being faithful. But you are also aware, worldly—you possess passion, humanity, vulnerability and strength. What a mistake people make who think you are, less than flesh and blood—or more!

You are visionary, you live in a world of secrets, intrigue, sensitivity. You exemplify poetic justice. At times you prefer symbols to facts, gestures to actions, smiles to laughter, the subtle raising of eyebrows to outright comment.

Pisces

You are one of the most charming, intriguing, downright sexy people on this planet, but the *illusion* is that you are aloof, unworldly, not even capable of standing the warm, racy thoughts that pulse through minds when, in a delicate gesture, you fire our imaginations. Make us see you as you are.

You are regarded by many as a poet. You are a dreamer who is capable, somehow, of dreaming dreams that not only can be seen, but heard and felt. You are, Pisces, able to get the feel of things. You are there, and aware. You inhale experience. You are in the thick of adventure. Pisces is protected, loved, sometimes scorned, but Pisces is there, aware, capable, strong in the face of adversity and, with it all, *gentle.*

I have said of you that it is not easy to define what you feel, but you *do* feel. Be sure to open yourself to these feelings, these impulses, for they are part of you. What I mean is that an open mind, an open heart, are requirements. Your creative urge is often camouflaged. Perhaps you feel depressed, unhappy sometimes. Then you open up, you give out; your creativity finds expression and you bubble over with energy, finally with joy.

But, listen: it is necessary for you to be quiet within. You gain strength through quiet meditation. You gain through periods of being alone. You must learn that being alone is not the same as being lonely. Instead, it is a way to store up creative energy.

You tend to become self-sacrificing in affairs of the heart. This isn't always good because, ultimately, it can lead to deep resentment. Yet, Pisces, you feel you must help, must dig deep to elevate the underdog . . . must dig deep to find gold. You get stepped on quite often. You suffer, you are humiliated, but your reward, you feel, is just around the corner. The ship is about to come in—*your* ship. As I say, you wait for your ship to come in but, inwardly, you sense it might be going in quite another direction. Listen, Pisces: you do things to yourself others wouldn't think of doing. You are philanthropic, but demanding. You are artistic, but conservative. You are musical in the sense that you have rhythm within your very being, but you are not always aware of discordant notes. You are self-indulgent where emotions are concerned. You are fascinated with distortion. At times some of you help this along through the use of drugs, alcohol: this being the negative side and adding up to self-abuse. You abhor pain but deliberately hurt yourself. You are capable but sometimes inept. You feet the drama of life, and the tragedy. You sense that life is funny in the tragic way that reality can be.

Listen, Pisces: you sense that there are important things to do, important people to know, great loves to experience. And you say, in effect . . . *it will happen* . . . in just a little while: give me a little more time. What you actually are pleading for, Pisces, is a respite—a delay, a postponement of the day when you must get your feet wet.

You love secrets. You respect confidences. But you tend to drift, to possess knowledge, yet to profess ignorance. Your motives may be very high, but you sometimes bury your head in the sand.

I want to wake you up, Pisces, to make you fully aware as well as sensitive, to get you going, to get the creative juices flowing. The future is apt to be meaningless if you tend to sway back and forth, back and forth, like a pendulum, going neither here nor there, but only sideways, keeping time, digging a rut in the air. The future then doesn't exist, nor do the opportunities, not does the romance, the poetry, and the song of life you hold so precious.

You see, Pisces, you tend to imagine people and situations as you so fervently wish they could be, and wishing, you seem to believe, will make it so. It doesn't. It only attracts people to you who will take what you give, and take some more, while you give, and hope and deceive yourself, until the shell becomes so thick you can't differentiate between *it* and the real you.

Recognize, Pisces, that you have a moral obligation not only to others—but to yourself. Your choice of friends, of people you love, can, at times, only be described as unworthy. You are sensitive, *capable* of producing fine, beautiful music. Yet you appear to *miss* the commercial twang, the rumble, and the noise of confusion. What must happen before you can be truly happy, Pisces, is that you must be self-reliant, not dependent on others, not used by others, not an easy mark for others. The famous astrologer and writer Alan Leo said of you: *Pisces people can nearly always be relied on—they are not always fully appreciated, for they will keep their talents in the background in a very unassuming way. Yet,* said Alan Leo, *they are inclined to worry too much, and are even obstinate. They are,* he said, *liable to intellectual folly which often springs from a gloomy and foreboding nature, owing to their not being properly understood.*

Listen, Pisces: you must shake yourself loose from emotional burdens which are not rightly your own. You have no need of cheapness, no need of suffering brought on by the selfishness, the coarseness, the inconsiderateness of others. Better to walk alone than to be abused, used, turned into an automaton who lives everyone else's life, experiences everyone else's troubles—better to be alone and hear the music of the spheres, better to be alone and *free*.

But, listen, Pisces: *once you make this decision you won't be alone*—not in the sense of being lonely. Once you throw off burdens which were not your own in the first place, your life will be full. It will contain the beauty of self-respect, and the respect and love others will grant you. You see, Pisces, you only create associates who don't respect you when you set them an example by appearing to think very little of yourself. Utilize your need for serving in a creative manner. Instead of waiting on the unworthy—entertain the world. Become part of an organization, institution, stage production. Put your thoughts on paper, the music of your moods into the form of a composition, a song. Whatever you do, don't bury your individuality—don't sink into the vast ocean of uselessness.

You have a way of smiling as if you were actually crying. Perhaps this is because Pisces has much to do with the theater, being the natural twelfth sign, and the two masks, one laughing, the other crying, are the symbols of the theater. Your smile one associates with a person who squints in order to get a better look, clearer vision. And, Pisces: you and I do know that often you laugh through tears. You may appear somewhat frail on occasion but you are capable of withstanding punishment. Your sense of humor is above average. You can be delightful, engaging, warm, passionate. And when you put the brakes on self-deception, when you see people and situations as they are, you will be pressing the gas pedal for life itself.

I think you know more than you tell, feel more than you reveal. Man or woman, you are capable of "quick study." This means you sum up, get the picture, perceive meanings almost instantaneously. While many of us are trying to decide, you are gaining a vision which, in due time, will become a reality—*your reality.*

Listen, I'm not trying to make you sound like some kind of mystic, although many mediums were born under Pisces. I am, however, trying to impart the impression that you receive nuances, hints, gestures as some others receive food and air and deliberate signals. You seem to know in *advance* what the final score will be. This can surprise you, at times, as much as it can startle the rest of us.

THE PISCES LOVER

Now, here are some secret hints for men about the women of Pisces. Listen, men: this woman appreciates kindness and consideration above almost anything else. You can win her by being sympathetic. If you want to be happy with a Pisces woman—don't hold back. No matter how terrible the truth, it is better to tell it. This lady, the Pisces woman, is a fighter as well as a poet. She has some secrets of her own, has some contacts or ideas that, if utilized, might well pull you out of difficulties. She is not an easy woman to understand—she often changes with the scenery, as if nature gave her a strange power to face any situation, no matter how pleasant or awful. You will want to shield her, protect her, but time and again she will prove that she is tough, able to take it. Then almost the next moment, she once more will become a gentle, amiable

Piscean. One of her great assets is a sense of humor; she will laugh when you most need to hear the sound of laughter. Give her confidence, warmth, and love—and you will be repaid doubly, triply. When dealing with the Pisces woman be frank, open, honest to the point of confiding your secrets. This appeals to her and gains her confidence. Once this is accomplished, she is not likely to fight your desires. The basis of this secret hint is to give the Pisces lady confidence in herself. She has a tendency toward self-doubt, sometimes expressed in a possessive attitude. But, given confidence, she loosens the reins, makes life more pleasant for herself—and for you.

Men, these women are extraordinary when it comes to psychic power. They can see through a falsehood. They can tell what the next move will bring. They can read your motives with crystal clarity.

Now, here are some secret hints for women about men born under Pisces. Go slow with this man. Don't push or force issues. Be subtle. Plan with care. Ingratiate yourself; make yourself a part of his work and life. He will soon look for you, ask your opinions, confide in you. He is a sensitive soul. He is not always the easiest man to be with, but he may well be one of the kindest and most considerate. Gentle methods can capture the Pisces man's heart. He does have a tendency to be self-indulgent. Forceful arguments can send him into a protective shell. The Pisces male is imaginative, often highly creative, and he is a dreamer. He is emotional, Neptunian, at times mediumistic in the sense that he appears to be inspired from out of the blue. He has flashes of insight and these first impressions are often not only correct, but ultimately prove profitable. This man is never completely contented. It is important to be aware of this fact. *It is a healthy discontent.* Often, he appears abstracted. You may be tempted to complain that there are problems he overlooks, to be attended to close at home. But, despite the distractions, despite the tendency to wander and to dream . . . once he decides he loves you . . . it is with all his heart. And he will seldom disappoint you when it comes to sympathy—or integrity.

YOUR RISING SIGN

All persons born under your sign are not exactly the same, although basic characteristics will hold. A horoscope, in actuality, is a map of the sky based on the time and place of birth. If you are aware of your birth time, here are some variations it may cause in your life and character:

Born between 4:00 and 6:00 A.M., your Rising Sign is apt to be Pisces, emphasizing the Neptunian influence. The double Neptune emphasis makes you more perceptive than the average native of your sign. Instead of indulging sometimes in mere illusion, you are analytical. You seek changes and you could have the reformer's zeal. You are capable of combining mysticism with reality; thus, you can be a writer, actor, hospital administrator. You can produce motion pictures. You can transform illusions into works of art. Your potential is tremendous and living up to it is your challenge.

Born between 6:00 and 8:00 A.M., your Ascendant is likely to be Aries, associated with the planet Mars. This combines with your Neptune significator to make you more active than the average native of your sign. You are energetic, but, frankly, proudly poetic in outlook. Your sense of originality is marked. You want your dreams, your writings, your ideas, and creations to be "on view." You are more direct than many under your sign, willing to take action so that what you dream becomes special and memorable. Your sense of knowing is a wonder. You are more subjective than objective, but you know how to make subjectivity practical. This, on the face of it, is contradictory. You are filled with contradictions: fiery, yet receptive, direct, but aware of the value of symbols. You are, to say the very least, unusual and your mark on the world can be definite, constructive.

Born between 8:00 and 10:00 A.M., your Ascendant is probably Taurus, associated with Venus. This combines with your Neptune Solar significator to make you more practical than the average native of your sign. You are not likely to hang on to people or situations for purely sentimental reasons. There is a purpose to much of what you do—a definite one. Your voice could be unusual; you compel people to listen, even when you are not saying anything particularly significant. You are not unwilling to tear down in order to rebuild. Your sense of beauty is magnified; you are sensuous. You are very attractive to the opposite sex and this could lead to complications. Mostly, though, you are intriguing, dramatic, and capable of fulfilling your basic ambitions.

Born between 10:00 A.M. and 12:00 noon, your Rising Sign is apt to be Gemini, giving you more of a sense of humor than the average native of your sign. You are versatile, provocative. Gemini is associated with Mercury. This combines with your Neptune indicator to make you more aware of long-range objectives than many who share your Solar sign. You are quick to decide, quick to laugh, quick to gesture, and quick to enlarge your views. Plainly, you are versatile, flexible, and open to challenge. You are restless, artistic, capable of articulating thoughts, visions. You are not likely to be satisfied with the status quo. Life, for you, is change. It should (in your belief) be fun. You are not a typical representative of your sign; there is more movement in your life and less introspection.

Born between 12:00 noon and 2:00 P.M., your Ascendant is likely to be Cancer, associated with the Moon. This combines with your Neptune significator to make you more moody, introspective, and intuitive than the average native of your sign. You attract people to you with their troubles. Many seem to regard you as a substitute mother or father. You are a combination of practicality and romanticism. You are more vague, however, about the present than you are concerning the future. This means that you are better at handling overall projects than details. You seem able to sense which properties, for example, will increase in value. Developing this sense could cause you to be a very rich romantic.

Born between 2:00 and 4:00 P.M., your Rising Sign is apt to be Leo, ruled by the Sun. This combines with your Neptune to make you dramatic, creative, and more positive about your views than is the average native of your sign. You can be stubborn in your insistence on "getting things done." Accomplishment is a key word with you. Your views can be fixed, but your principles are also stable. You are regal, you possess an air that makes people aware of your presence. Your statements can sound like pronouncements. Self-expression is a necessity for you. You do better working for yourself than for others. Your timing is good, often bordering on the dramatic. And you attract the opposite sex without half trying.

Born between 4:00 and 6:00 P.M., your Ascendant is likely to be Virgo, associated with Mercury. This combines with your Neptune Solar indicator to make you more concise than is the average native of your sign. You are quick, have a way of telling others what's best for them without being offensive. You are good at figuring odds; you take calculated risks and, most often, succeed. You are perceptive, attracted to medicine, health aids, and sincerely desire to help alleviate suffering. You are capable of handling details. You are imaginative, but know when to keep your feet on the ground. You can be specific, but you also are aware of the abstract. You could be a bit more flexible, but generally you can see many sides of a question.

Born between 6:00 and 8:00 P.M., your Rising Sign is apt to be Libra, ruled by Venus. This combines with your Neptune significator to make you more artistic than the average native of your sign. You can put images on paper. You can transform dreams into something solid. You can explain your views in a manner which enables others to perceive your meanings. You are a seeker of justice and balance. You tend to veer away from extremes. You can design, create in a scientific or orderly way, which is not always the case with those who share your sign. You are a good host or hostess; you put people at their ease by expressing genuine interest in their pursuits, opinions.

Born between 8:00 and 10:00 P.M., your Ascendant or Rising Sign is likely to be Scorpio, associated with Pluto. This combines with your Neptune Solar significator to make you more intuitive, more willing to share your views and knowledge than is the average native of your sign. You tend to feel that you know what is best. Thus, you express your views in a positive manner. You are a teacher, an individual who comes back from an exploration to explain his findings. Some find you aggressive. Others appreciate your forthright manner. You can be subtle. You are capable of keeping secrets, especially where money is involved. You tell what you know, but you can do so in a manner designed to camouflage some key factors. You have inhibitions, but you expect others to be completely frank. In this sense, you might be a dilemma—not only to others, but to yourself.

Born between 10:00 P.M. and 12:00 midnight, your Ascendant is likely to be Sagittarius, associated with Jupiter. This combines with your Neptune significator to make you more forthright, frank, open-minded than is the average native of your sign. You are independent, original in your approach to most problems. You can an appear selfish because very little is needed to irritate you if you are deterred from your basic goal. You know where you want to go—and why. Some think your view is narrow. Those people do not have a true understanding of your nature. You think of a promise as sacred and will do all in your power to fulfill it. You are more ambitious than many born under your sign. You are unique; you can be fiery and display enthusiasm, while at the same time appearing to be easygoing. This puzzles many and, although you are attractive to the opposite sex, many claim they find it impossible really to know you.

Born between 12:00 midnight and 2:00 A.M., your Rising Sign is apt to be Capricorn, ruled by Saturn. This combines with your Neptune Solar significator to make you more aware of domestic responsibilities than is the average native of your sign. You are fond of art, music, drama. But your creative endeavors usually are kept within a practical framework. You are responsible, you take seriously your obligations. At times, you display a tendency to be morose. But new clothes, different surroundings, good food, a bright companion can "bring you out of yourself." Your feelings are not always apparent, but you are basically an affectionate individual. You are much concerned with opportunities for members of your family, especially the youngsters. You are an advocate of education and lean toward the liberal arts. Law concerns you and so does justice. You do not feel the two are always analogous.

Born between 2:00 and 4:00 A.M., your Rising Sign or Ascendant is apt to be Aquarius, associated with Uranus. This combines with your Neptune significator to make you more of a "practical visionary" than is the average native of your sign. You are inventive. You can foresee trends. You are dynamic. You are capable of improving the lot of all of us. But, at times, you overlook the needs of those closest to you. You are better at perceiving what will be than always understanding how to cope with what actually exists. Your personal magnetism attracts many; you can recommend the right person at the right time. In other words, you handle emergencies in a cool, efficient manner. But everyday problems tend to bore you.

PISCES FRIENDS AND PARTNERS

Your relationship to another Piscean can produce good results, provided you both possess the determination to give form to thoughts, dreams, ambitions. With another Pisces, there are changes and there could be travel. You become more analytical; two Pisceans can create products that bring joy as well as serve utilitarian purposes. Generally, the relationship is favorable.

You are physically attracted to people born under Cancer; your sign is well-aspected to Cancer, Scorpio, Capricorn, and Taurus. Pisces is not favorably aspected to Gemini, Sagittarius, or Virgo. Your sign is considered neutral in relation to Aquarius, Aries, Leo, and Libra.

PISCES CAREERS

The Tenth House of a horoscope has to do, among other things, with career, ambitions, prestige, standing in the community, and general success through occupational efforts. The Tenth Sector of your Solar horoscope is Sagittarius, associated with the planet Jupiter. With Sagittarius on the cusp of your Tenth House, you are individualistic, sensitive, capable of capturing the moods of the public. Above almost all else, you are an individual; your own style, your own imprint, your originality, your uniqueness must mark your occupational efforts.

You want your tone, your voice, your imprint to spread; self-expression is almost a way of life with you. And that's the way it is with you in connection with your career. The only prestige you recognize is the kind that gives you recognition for yourself, not for any imitation.

Motion pictures, the theater, and television are outstanding for you in the occupational field; the ability to write and publish is there; your drive is strong toward poetry or poetic prose.

Many outstanding artists are among your zodiacal kin. Van Gogh, Renoir, and Michelangelo are a few examples. Your sense of harmony finds an outlet in music, too. Rimski-Korsakov was a Piscean and so was Caruso. Art, music, writing, and other activities stemming from an urge to give of one's self are associated with Pisces. Victor Hugo had the Sun in your sign. Longfellow and Elizabeth Barrett Browning also were Pisceans.

You are attracted to the occult; many mediums, as I mentioned, are Pisceans. Religion and metaphysics draw you. You are also attracted to language and research, to the sea or to work where imagination is a basic necessity.

Occupations associated with your sign also include: detective, anesthetist, distiller, naval officer, and executive in a sanitarium, museum, or library. Work associated with solitude also attracts you. You are capable of being alone without being lonely.

Add these occupational possibilities: dancer, chemical engineer, deep-sea diver, oceanographer, oil executive, organic chemist, photographer, and shoe manufacturer.

THE PISCES HAND

Some astrologers are proficient at guessing Sun signs; that is, they can look at an individual and perceive his, or her, zodiacal sign. This is no easy task—it requires experience, practice. The reason is that the Rising Sign (at the time and place of birth) affects personality and appearance, as does the sign the Moon occupied at birth. Yet, the place of the Sun is a strong indicator where character and appearance enter the picture.

Over the years, I have found that one significant key in this effort is the human hand. A person's hand often reveals whether that individual was born under a Fire, Earth, Air, or Water Sign.

You, Pisces, were born under a Water Sign; Pisces belongs to the Water element. The Water-type band is generally oval-shaped. The mount, under the thumb, is fleshy, well-developed. The Mount of Luna, under the little finger and near the wrist, is also highly developed, denoting sensitivity and imagination. (Water trinity people are those born under Pisces, Scorpio, and Cancer.) The palm is fleshy; the fingers are usually thick; the hand is soft, similar to the Air Sign hand. These hands, of the Water element, denote people who are impressionable, probably psychic, and capable of capturing moods via painting, writing, or other creative endeavors.

Study the eleven other *Astrological Revelations* in this volume for information about other hands. Your skill at guessing Sun signs via a study of hands will develop with practice if it interests you.

PISCES SECRETS

The horoscope, with its twelve angles or Houses, covers every area of life, including your secrets. The Twelfth House holds sway over secret fears, fantasies, undercover problems, all that is hidden or beneath the surface.

In your case, Aquarius occupies the Twelfth House; the Uranus of Aquarius combines with your Neptune significator to show that one of your secrets is a strong desire for recognition—*on a grand scale.*

You may appear to be sensitive, delicate. In many ways, you are. But your secret desire is to be strong enough to gain universal recognition, to appeal to the masses. This is almost the opposite of the face you show to the world. You continue to want to be (and you are) unique. But you fear (one of your secrets) that this very uniqueness will limit your appeal. The key is to be unique, and to get rid of the fear. That's easy to say, but it can be easy to accomplish, too. Be yourself, not consciously concerned with the reception your work or efforts will receive.

One of your secrets is a desire for popularity. You could appear to be a "loner." But you want friends—you want to be accepted—you have fantasies that your hopes and wishes will become realities, and be shared with brilliant, sensitive, creative people. Listen: in your fantasies, you are lionized. What Leo appears to be outwardly, you are inwardly. That's one of your major secrets or fantasies.

You are, in that inward world that is so much a part of you, popular and sexy, friendly and extroverted. You want to finish, to be the "last word." This is not in the sense of having the last word in an argument. It is in the sense of being the "last word" in your area: an authority, applauded, called the "master," regarded as one to consult.

Listen: one of your secrets is that you secretly are something of a psychiatrist. You want people to come to you with their problems. You want to analyze, deduct, and be a "medicine" to the emotional wounds suffered by the world. You do this through art and/or creative endeavors. You also do it by being an excellent *listener.*

Although you regard your private life as not only private, but sacred, your secret wish is to be interrupted. That is, one of your secret desires is not to go into a reverie without being interrupted by those seeking counsel.

In your secret life, the world is Uranian, that is, filled with symbols, astrological symbols perhaps, maybe psychological, dream, or other symbols. The reality is that dreams and problems, on any level, can be solved by *your interpretations.*

You seldom nourish "wicked" secrets. You have sexual fantasies. But you do not harbor secret desires to do injury to others. Your secrets involve friendship and love, not violence.

Your major secret is an intense desire to be consulted. You want to be in a sense hermetically sealed, but still available to those whom you regard as special and unique-to those who love you, and to those to whom you can offer not only consolation and love, but genuine *solutions.*

Your secrets, Pisces, are a part of you, more so than is usually true of natives of the other zodiacal signs, because Pisces belongs to that section of the chart actually related to secrets.